100

FREE WAYS TO HAPPIER DAYS!

Achieve Happiness.

CATHY SHUTER

BALBOA.
PRESS

A DIVISION OF HAY HOUSE

Balboa Press books may be ordered through booksellers or by contacting:

Balboa Press
A Division of Hay House
1663 Liberty Drive
Bloomington, IN 47403
www.balboapress.com
1 (877) 407-4847

Because of the dynamic nature of the Internet, any web addresses or links contained in this book may have changed since publication and may no longer be valid. The views expressed in this work are solely those of the author and do not necessarily reflect the views of the publisher, and the publisher hereby disclaims any responsibility for them.

The author of this book does not dispense medical advice or prescribe the use of any technique as a form of treatment for physical, emotional, or medical problems without the advice of a physician, either directly or indirectly. The intent of the author is only to offer information of a general nature to help you in your quest for emotional and spiritual well-being. In the event you use any of the information in this book for yourself, which is your constitutional right, the author and the publisher assume no responsibility for your actions.

Any people depicted in stock imagery provided by Thinkstock are models, and such images are being used for illustrative purposes only.
Certain stock imagery © Thinkstock.

Print information available on the last page.

ISBN: 978-1-5043-4075-5 (sc)
ISBN: 978-1-5043-4076-2 (e)

Balboa Press rev. date: 09/29/2015

This book is dedicated to my Gran Mary Muston who has always loved, supported me and encouraged me to follow my dreams.

Be Happy

All too often people drag themselves through life. They get up in the morning, go to work and then fall asleep at night. They may not feel happy but then again they don't exactly feel sad. I believe that we owe it to ourselves to lead full and happy lives. Sometimes we forget to make time for the things that we enjoy. '100 Free Ways...' is intended to encourage you to start prioritising your happiness. You can do this today!

'100 Free Ways...' is dedicated to highlighting the good things in life and to helping people realise that finding things that make us happy needn't cost a fortune. My aim is to show you things that you can try right now to help you to feel happier.

We all have dreams and in life we experience highs and lows. My life has been exciting lately. I have changed my job and moved house. I have become a Life Coach and have finally found the commitment and courage needed to start writing in earnest. I have always thought of myself as an author. As a young person I wrote short stories. I even sent some manuscripts off to some publishers to see if they would accept them.

When I was young I had confidence in my writing abilities. The publishers rejected my work and like many other people I got distracted by other things in life and so I put this writing dream of mine on hold. I told myself I needed to "grow up and get a proper job."

I did this but I never completely forgot my childhood wish. My writing goal was 'in storage' but not abandoned completely. The fact that you are reading this today is living proof that I finally did breathe life back into my dream. You can realise your dreams too.

Here are 100 thoughts, ideas and suggestions for you. Some ideas may appeal more than others. That's OK. Pick out the good bits and leave the parts that don't interest you. These suggestions will help anyone open-minded and willing enough to listen to new ideas. I hope that reading this book will benefit you and give you the self confidence needed to follow your own dreams. There are changes that you can make in your life right away. They cost little or no money to put the into place. Give them a try and change your life for the better.

The First Step:

One day I stopped procrastinating and decided to start changing my life and keep on changing it until I was happy with it. I was experiencing many areas of frustration at the time. This included financial struggle and lack of job satisfaction. I realised that if I wanted change then I was the person that needed to change. Instead of walking around muttering to myself about the unfairness of it all I decided to examine the areas of my life that I wanted to improve. I looked for guidance to help me make the necessary changes. I found help in all sorts of unexpected places.

I have had an interest in personal development for a long time and had been reading books on the subject for years. I found self-help books to be helpful during challenging periods of my life. Reading them was a good way of exploring my concerns without having to admit to anyone that I had any problems. I have always been quite a private person when it comes to sharing my fears. I prefer to 'put on a brave face' and get on with things. Reading the books helped me to clarify what was wrong. I liked some of the tips and the self-improvement suggestions. In truth, I got a bit addicted to reading self- help books. I would read one book, find a useful tip and consider it until the novelty wore off. The book would lose some of its initial appeal. I would place it on a bookshelf along with those that had gone before and forget all about it. Later on another book would catch my eye. I would buy it, read it, think about it and move on.

One day I realised that if I really wanted change I needed to set goals to achieve that change and then act. Taking action was what was missing. From then on personal development books helped to guide and inspire me to set goals and then I knew my job was to act. Things really started improving for me after that.

My interest in personal development progressed to watching DVD's, listening to CD's and attending webinars. Webinars are freely available on The Internet. It was while watching a DVD that I first discovered vision boards. They are the first things I want you to consider. They can help you to make your life happier.

1.   Vision Boards:

We all have goals and dreams if we allow ourselves to have them. Many of us keep our dreams to ourselves and don't truly believe they will come true. If we are clear about what we want and believe that we deserve good things then our dreams are much more likely to manifest.

Vision boards are an excellent visual way of representing our goals and dreams. They are a powerful way of helping you to clearly set out the things you wish for in life. These wishes might range from hoping for a set of beautiful new clothes to achieving better health, more wealth and happiness.

A vision board acts as a kind of pictorial shopping list. You think carefully about what you like, picture it clearly in your mind then find or draw pictures of what you desire. You cut out the pictures, arrange them onto some card and you have your vision board.

Look at your vision board daily. Look carefully at each image and imagine having those things right now. How do you feel? Allow yourself to really feel as if they are surrounding you now. Do this every day. Believe that they are on their way to you now and you will be surprised how quickly events can set themselves in motion to bring you closer to reaching your goals.

Life has a funny way of offering you exactly the opportunities you need in order to achieve your goals. Your role at this stage is to be alert and to seize the opportunities when they present themselves to you. To help the vision board to 'work its magic' consider taking photo's of the things you wish for and then upload them onto your computer. Put them to music you find inspiring. That way you have a visual reminder of your dreams that will help you to focus more vividly on your goals.

I have been using vision boards for a few years now and it is great to look back at them and see the lovely things that have entered my life. It is almost like watching the pictures come to life in front of my very eyes. Successes have included me passing my driving test and getting a new job when I really needed one. Why not give them a try? I think you will be delighted at the results.

2.   Affirmations:

Along with vision boards I have found affirmations to be a powerful way of making positive changes in my life. Affirmations are stated in the present tense. You say them out loud regularly to yourself. An example of a wonderfully positive affirmation is:

"Everything is happening exactly as it should."

When I say it, this really helps to remind me that difficult times are a necessary part of our lives to help move us forward. I say this affirmation to myself daily and it prompts me to take life as it comes. It helps me to stop worrying when I perceive that things are going wrong. It even helps me to realise that things may not be going wrong at all. Rather than going wrong, events are working out in new and unexpected ways.

Life is a journey with all kinds of twists and turns and while something challenging is happening it can feel like 'the end of the world' but a few days later when you look back on the incident you often realise that it was not as bad as you had thought. You can choose any positive affirmations you like: "My life is getting better and better," or "I love myself as I am."

It is important not to say anything you aren't yet quite ready to believe. If you are trying to lose weight saying: 'I have a wonderful, slim body' may not resonate with you.

Instead you could say, "My body is getting healthier each day."

You can add positive affirmations to your vision boards and you can write them on scraps of paper. Post them in places where you will see them around your home. If you see them and read them often enough, your subconscious mind starts to take the message on board. It will begin to actively look out for evidence to support your statement. Gradually you will begin to truly believe in these statements and this will enhance your life enormously.

At this point take some time to notice what you are saying to yourself. Many people are internally very critical of themselves and carry out a lot of negative self-talk. The subconscious mind will take on board these negative statements and look for further evidence to support them. It is very important to think the best of yourself and to make the most of the good things you do have going for you in life.

If you find this rather difficult then try listing three things you like about yourself. If you really struggle to do this ask people around you to tell you what they like about you. If someone says you are funny or helpful, for example, you can turn these comments into positive affirmations.

As you do this your subconscious mind will begin to tune in to other positive things that people say about you and you can also turn these comments into positive affirmations. This will help you to truly celebrate the wonderful, unique person you are.

3. Meditation:

I am a chatty, out-going person or at least I am quite a lot of the time. In reality I can also be quite thoughtful and shy at times. As a result, I prefer interacting in small groups rather than facing crowds. I enjoy meaningful conversations with others. I am genuinely interested in what other people have to say and yet I am sometimes uncomfortable with silences. I ask myself, why is this? I think it has to do with the fact that silent spaces allow a gap for my negative self-talk to chip in. When there is a silence I sometimes tell myself the other person must be getting bored and that is why they are not responding to me.

When I am on my own, my mind offers up a constant stream of babble. I become aware of my thoughts and consciously observe what is being said. Invariably my mind appears to be throwing up all kinds of self-doubts and anxieties.

It can be very helpful to take time to listen to what you are saying to yourself. If it appears negative for a significant amount of the time then it can be very beneficial to address this.

Meditation is a very helpful way of reducing the seemingly ceaseless chatter in your mind. When I meditate it helps me to find a way of quietening my mind.

Breathing deeply and relaxing are important first steps. Start by finding a quiet and comfortable place to sit or lie down where you won't be disturbed. Being still for a period of time, allowing thoughts to enter then leave your head can really help to reduce stress and help you to feel happier. It is definitely worth trying even for a few moments.

Guided meditation with accompanying tranquil music, helps me to stay focussed. Deepak Chopra and Oprah Winfrey regularly team up to offer free guided meditation sessions. Each day has a theme. One day it might be 'achieving happiness' and another day it may be 'finding wisdom.' Each has an associated mantra.

A mantra is a word that you repeat silently to aid your meditation. Repeating the word over and over to yourself helps you to concentrate on the meditation rather than becoming distracted by your thoughts and physical sensations. These sessions are run on a regular basis. They are free of charge so you could try them for yourself to see if these sessions would work for you.

Try it and you are likely to find meditating gently uplifting and incredibly relaxing. There are a lot of meditations freely available when you search The Internet. Experiment with some and find the ones you enjoy.

Regular meditation really can transform your life. If I can do it you can do it! Meditation brings me peace that I have never experienced before. It has opened my mind enough to be receptive to a range of other useful techniques as well. I believe that it will do the same for you.

4.   The Power of Now:

I spend a lot of time worrying about what I have done in the past or what might happen in the future. I know this does not serve me but it is a very hard habit to break. Is this something you do too?

Rarely does anything truly scary happen in the present.

A disproportionate amount of precious time is spent needlessly worrying. I fret about things that happened, that might have happened but didn't and what may or may not happen in the future.

If I am totally focused on the present when something bad happens, I am in the best possible position to act quickly and effectively, in order to minimise the impact of an incident. If I am concentrating on my driving and notice a car hurtling towards me, for example, I can swerve out of the way. If I am driving along lost in thoughts about things that may never happen I may not even notice the car before it is too late. This is just one example of the importance of living in the moment.

I realise that it is difficult to remain in the present. In the moments when I am fully present my senses feel fully alert and I am full of life. The more I am able to focus on Now the better the quality of my life experience. I am more appreciative of my surroundings and the people around me. I am not saying that we should deny our past or fail to act to prevent difficulty in the future. Instead I am suggesting that we take time to appreciate the moment we have right now. Now is the only time that truly counts. The past is past and the future is not certain. Now is our real gift.

Try spending your life living as much as possible in the present tense. When you find your mind wandering into the past or the future, take time to absorb your surroundings. Listen to the birds singing, look at the flowers and feel the breeze cooling your face. Take a deep breath and truly enjoy this precious life. Love the life that is yours right here, right now. This is a technique that costs nothing and the benefits can be tremendous.

5. Subconscious Mind:

It is useful to think of your mind as made up of two parts. Your conscious and your subconscious mind. The conscious mind is the part that you are aware of. You make up your mind to do something or stop doing something like choosing to give up smoking, for example. You have willpower. You buy a nicotine patch and are determined to quit.

Your subconscious mind lurks beneath the surface. It runs many parts of your body on autopilot without you having to think about it. It also tries to protect you. To do this it remembers all the positive and the negative things that have happened to you including the remarks that people have made to you. In order to keep you safeguarded it works to prevent you from taking risks or doing anything that might hurt you.

Maybe the last time you tried giving up smoking you felt lousy so you gave up trying, for example. Perhaps you then felt disappointed in yourself for giving up on quitting. Your subconscious mind is reluctant to let you go through that pain again and has been gathering evidence from your world to remind you of the difficulties involved in quitting smoking. Your subconscious mind works away at you, gradually eroding your resolve so that your willpower quickly dries up and you give up trying.

Your subconscious mind stores everything it hears about you. This includes all the negative self-talk which turns into your very own limiting self-beliefs. You may start to tell yourself that you will never be able to quit smoking so you give up trying. This can happen without you being consciously aware of it.

The good news is that you can start to re-programme your subconscious mind by using positive affirmations. Set small, clear and achievable goals and enlist the support of trusted friends. This can help you to change any unhelpful habits that you may have developed.

If you tell your subconscious mind kindly and firmly that you are a non-smoker and that you no longer need cigarettes, gradually after frequent repetitions of this affirmation your subconscious mind will begin to absorb the message and begin to look out for evidence to support it. If you can encourage your subconscious mind to work with your conscious mind you have a recipe for success!

6. Making Tiny Changes.

Small is good. If you have a big goal that you would like to achieve then aim to identify a set of small, achievable steps that you can take in order to achieve your goal. Setting a huge goal and going all out to achieve it in one go can be intimidating.

Trying to achieve a large goal all at once can feel overwhelming and put you off trying at all. Let us imagine that you are in debt and you wish to become debt free. Short of winning money, begging, borrowing or stealing, you are unlikely to be able to totally achieve this goal overnight. If you can take one small step towards your goal each day it will be possible for you to achieve your goal a little at a time. You will worry less and act more.

There is a Chinese proverb which says that. "One step at a time is good walking."

I really relate to this. Take one step and then the next will be easier. The first step is often the hardest. Once you move in the right direction it is much easier to maintain progress. After a time, encouraged by your progress, you will be able to look back and see the ground that you have covered.

If we return to the debt example, a useful first step would be to identify an accurate figure, how much money do you actually owe? It can be hard to admit this to yourself but this is a necessary step to acknowledge if you are serious about debt reduction. Let us imagine that you owe £20,000.

Once you admit this to yourself then the next step would be to work out who the money is owed to and what are the priority payments. By this I mean it is essential to ensure you pay your rent or mortgage or you may lose your home and so these payments must be prioritised. While important, energy suppliers may be willing to accept a reduced payment as part of a payment plan if you negotiate with them. Perhaps the £500 you borrowed from your uncle may be paid back a little later if you ask him nicely. It would be helpful to try to identify how you ended up in debt in the first place. Was there a one off event or a set of circumstances that contributed to the debt? What action can you take now and in the future to prevent yourself getting into further financial difficulty?Look at your income and your outgoings to see how much is left over at the end of the month. It may be that making savings by switching utility supplier will help you so that you have a little money left at the end of each month that can be put towards debt repayment.

Once you have been able to make some savings, it may also be possible to make some extra money by taking a second job or by selling unwanted items. Some of us are good at making things and may be able to make and sell original items. There are all kinds of imaginative ways that people have managed to turn a hobby into a successful business, for example. When you take action you feel less 'frozen' and less scared of your debt. Once you reduce your fear, there is more room in your mind for you to start thinking and acting more creatively.

I have found that this approach works well with a whole range of challenges.

First you identify the problem. Next you work out what has happened to help put you in this situation in the first place. Then you consider what tiny actions can you take now to resolve the situation and what can you do in the future to reduce the likelihood of this challenge occurring again.

Once you are thinking creatively, you are much more likely to be inspired by new people and ideas. If you are worried that a tiny step will make little difference, remember that a captain steers their ship by moving the tiller. If they move the tiller a little too far in one direction, they will find that over time they have steered way off course. Once they realise this they only need to make tiny adjustments in order to correct their course.

I hope this will help you to realise that small and simple actions taken over time, can make a huge difference to your life. They can help you to change for the better. Equally if you think you have strayed off course in your life it only takes small but regular adjustments for you to get to where you want to be.

7.   Achieving Balance:

It has taken me a long time to realise that achieving balance in your life is an incredibly important thing.

For a person to be happy they often seek positive relationships, enough money to live on, a rewarding job or role in life. They seek to be fit, healthy and free from excessive stress. Some people have good relationships but are experiencing financial hardship while others are rich but feel unfit and unwell.

Lack in one area often has a negative impact on other areas of your life, eventually. For example, if you have little money, this can eventually have a negative impact on family life. You are unable to afford to do things together and this may cause you to drift apart.

If you feel that one or more areas of your life is being neglected it is time to remedy this. Set a small, achievable goal to help improve the situation today. Once you have taken action in one area of your life and you start to see improvements, then you can reassess the other areas of your life and see what needs attention next. It may be that you feel that you are neglecting your family at the moment and so you resolve to leave work earlier one day per week. This has the positive outcome of you being able to spend more quality time with your family. Improving your work life balance also helps you to feel happier and may even improve your ability to complete tasks at work as you are more relaxed and focussed. This means that even though you are spending less time at work you are able to work more efficiently and get more done when you are there.

If one area of your life is neglected it is not long before this has a negative impact on other areas of your life. If you are neglecting your diet you may become overweight and this will increase your chances of becoming ill. This could cause you to take time off work and you could lose out on pay which would adversely affect your family life. Can you see how this becomes a vicious circle? By taking action in one area you can break this cycle.

8.   The Power of Positive Thinking.
('Thoughts are Things.')

Positive thinking works.

Thinking positively does not require you to deny the things that are happening around you, instead you look for the most positive outcome in any given situation. If you think negatively a lot, then your attention is absorbed by all the things that could possibly go wrong. The World then appears to be a corrupt, unfair and damaged place but if you look carefully amidst all the gloom and the doom you will see that there between the cracks of that grey, concrete paving slab, a beautiful, wild flower has emerged! Look around you. Examine the things around you carefully and I am sure that you can spot at least one positive thing everywhere you look. You might want a brand new car but at least your 'old banger' has passed its MOT and you can go wherever you want to go.

Whenever I make the effort to think positively I find that new opportunities start to come my way. If a letter arrives in my letter-box, before I open it I remind myself that the news is likely to be good or at least neutral. I open the letter and my prediction is often right.

I spent years assuming the worst and then one day I made a conscious decision to expect the best and the quality of my life has improved significantly as a result. You may wonder why this might be. There are a number of explanations for this – one possible explanation is the 'Law of Attraction.' It is said that this is the law which states that 'Like attracts like.'

If you think positive thoughts and focus on positive things then positive events are more likely to make their way to you. If you think about this it does make sense. Imagine if you are happy, alert and walking along in the rain, you are more likely to spot that £10 floating in the puddle in front of you than if you are stamping along muttering to yourself about the lousy weather. When you think positively, you are more likely to be open to the new ideas and opportunities that are offered to you. They are yours for the taking when you start to notice them.

In a programme featuring Derren Brown, two people were offered exactly the same opportunities. The positive thinker won out. The negative thinker assumed everyone that was trying to help them was in fact trying to rip them off and so he ended up no better off than he had been at the beginning of the programme. The positive thinker ended up with more money and a flourishing business because they gratefully accepted the opportunities offered to them.

9. Pay It Forward: Random Acts Of Kindness

Have you heard of 'Pay It Forward?' It is a wonderful way of doing something nice for people and it makes you feel good too. I was using Facebook recently and a friend posted that she was looking for 5 people to give her their contact details. At some point in the following year she would be able to send a surprise, such as a postcard, a theatre ticket or anything else that she felt would make the recipient happy. In return the recipient would ask for 5 people to give them their contact details so that they could do the same for some other people. I signed up to this initiative and was delighted to receive my surprise. I think it is a great idea and I had great fun choosing gifts for the 5 people who gave me their details.

I also see 'Pay It Forward' working in other ways. Whenever I go out of my way to do something for someone while expecting nothing in return I feel good. I try to do what I can for people, whether it be getting shopping for an elderly neighbour or giving a work colleague a nice card to cheer them up when they are feeling down.

At other times when I am having a hard time, other people have done lovely things to help me. At one time I was really struggling financially. One of my work colleagues picked up on the fact that I had no money to replace my vacuum cleaner which had packed up earlier in the week. I had to resort to sweeping the entire house with a dustpan and brush. Without saying a word she had a whip-round at work and I was presented with a brand new vacuum cleaner! I was unbelievably touched by this kind gesture.

I think that this is how the world works best. You do what you can to help when you can and when you are in need others will step in to help you.

The Random Acts Of Kindness Foundation also inspires people to be kind to others and is definitely worth getting involved in. People from all around the world think of ways that they can make life better for others. Both web pages are well worth a visit and are featured below:

https://www.randomactsofkindness.org/
http://payitforwardday.com/

10. Difficult People as Teachers:

Do you sometimes find that wherever you work there seems to be one or two people who really seem to be trying to show you up or deliberately trying to annoy you? From time to time I have found that things are going well in my life but there seems to be someone who manages to bring down my mood and make me look silly. I admit that it can be easy to resent people like that but recently I have realised that if someone sparks this kind of reaction in me they often have something valuable to teach me.

When someone criticises me now, I try to listen to what they are saying and fully consider if there is any truth in what they are saying. If they do have a point I can thank them for their feedback and learn from what they have said. If I consider what they are saying carefully and there seems to be no truth in what they are saying I can still say, "Maybe you are right."

Challenging people don't expect you to react in this way as they are expecting a disagreement and when they don't get one they are likely to walk away and leave you to get on with your day.

Sometimes people can come across as pushy or bossy at first but when you get to know them you alter your opinion when you discover their good qualities.

Sometimes we clash with people because they are very different from us and have a different life experience. If you take time to listen to the views of people who are different from you it is possible to discover new insights. Sometimes we struggle with people because they are too similar to us. They demonstrate our character traits and this can be difficult for us to acknowledge.

Getting to know and understand people that we find difficult at first can be a very rewarding experience. They can teach us a lot about ourselves, our reactions and the way we see the world.

11. Gratitude:

One of the most effective ways I know of boosting my happiness is listing the things that I am grateful for every day. I start by writing the words, 'I am so thankful for' and then I list 10 of the things that I am grateful for today. I also express the reasons why I am grateful. I might write, 'I am so grateful for my dog Ollie as his antics make me laugh every day!' Once I have listed ten things I look back over them and realise that I have a many great things going on in my life.

Once I began this I started to find more and more things to be grateful for. I even managed to do this the day I had a serious car accident as I found that there were so many people willing to help me on that day, from The Emergency Services to concerned passers by. The whole experience left me feeling overwhelmed with gratitude that there are so many kind, caring people in the world.

When you start listing the things that you are grateful for you become increasingly appreciative of the incredible things that you have in your life and before you know it even more wonderful things find their way to you.

Even if I decide that I would like something new, a new sofa for example, I start from a position of gratitude for the sofa that I already have and the fact that it is cosy, comfortable and well made. Starting from a position of gratitude really helps me to appreciate how lucky I am and when I feel appreciative it is incredible how more new and exciting opportunities start to find their way to me. If you don't believe me then try it for yourself!

'Ollie reminds me to have fun.'

12. Present Tense Manifestations:

A very effective way of attracting new things into your life is to create a vivid picture of what you would like in your mind then imagine that you already have them. To help you to do this you can write down the details, draw them even.

If I decided that I would like a new home, for example, I would be very specific. How large would I like my home to be? How many bedrooms would it have? What would the stairs look like? What colour are the carpets? I would look through catalogues and find furniture to go in the house. What is the garden like? I would choose the bedding plants from a catalogue. I would look around the shops and choose the curtains and cutlery. I would tell myself that the house was already mine. I would bring the house to life!

Once I have a clear picture of my house I express gratitude for the home I actually do have and appreciate all the happy times I have spent here. I then vividly imagine moving into my new home. I picture booking the removal van, packing everything into boxes, letting the bank know my new address. I allow myself to feel the excitement of moving home, the tension of Moving Day, the tiredness after unpacking all the boxes. Feeling the emotions helps to make it feel real.

Once my dream house is fixed firmly in my mind I am ready to take action in order to make my dream a reality. Lots of little actions help to set the wheels in motion. This worked for me when I decided I did want to move house. Clearing out my house, throwing away all the unwanted junk, selling items at a boot-air helped me to prepare for Moving Day. These actions all counted towards my goal.

Every day I pictured my new home in my mind, allowed myself to feel the emotions and take the small but steady actions that moved me towards my goal.

I know that it is important to keep an open mind and to accept opportunities that may present themselves to me that will help me move faster towards achieving my dreams.

This exercise links well with the idea of creating vision boards as vision boards are a practical way of helping us vividly picture our dreams. Try it for yourself.

13. Beauty of Nature:

Go outside. It doesn't matter what the weather is like. Go into the countryside if at all possible and look around you. Look at the trees, the grass and the sky. Take a deep breath. Feel the fresh air entering your body. Listen carefully to the sounds. Can you hear the birds?

Are there dogs barking? If you listen carefully, can you hear the breeze?

Take time out of your life and spend it in the countryside. If you can't do that then consider going to a park or walking to a place near your home that has a pretty garden. Even if you are house-bound you can open the window, enjoy the breeze entering your room and enjoy the scenery outside.

Once you are in the country or as close as you can get to it you can sit down or you can take off your shoes and stand barefoot on the earth. You can go for a walk, absorb everything that you see around you.

Go out whenever you get the chance. Find your favourite place and return there as often as you can. Even when you are not there you can picture that special place in your mind. You could even take photographs and display them in your home. Take pictures or imagine the trees, the grass, the birds and the clouds in the sky. Picture the scene as vividly as you can in your imagination. Whenever you are feeling under stress, if you cannot actually go and unwind in the countryside you can always imagine being there. If you cannot go outside at all then get someone to go out and take photographs of beautiful scenery especially for you. Have the photographs framed and display them where you can clearly see them.

Take in your surroundings, absorb every detail. Even if you live in a busy city, Nature isn't far away.

Look at the sunset. Lie in bed and listen to the sounds of the storm. Can you hear the rain pounding and the thunder crashing? Watch the flash of lightening illuminate your room.

I believe that Nature is grounding. It puts you in touch with the things that are really important in life.

As you walk in Nature, take in the seasons, the colours, the fresh green of Spring, the mellow yellow of Summer, the reds and golds of Autumn and the spectacular silvers of Winter.

Listen to the crackle of the falling leaves as you wander through them and the crunch of the snow as you walk down a frosty path. Each season has its own beauty and keeps you in touch with reality.

'Explore beautiful places.'

14. Pets as Teachers:

I have learnt such a lot from animals. I once had a rescue-cat I nicknamed Fisher as she somehow ended up with a rather long grand-sounding name: Princess Ginger Kiara the First. Fisher was a tiny but determined ginger cat. She came to live with my family when she was seven months old. She was fiercely independent and kept all the other cats firmly out of her garden, many of whom were twice her size! She was graceful and efficient in her movements, planning her every step. She used to follow me all around the house.

Fisher was certainly a creature of routine and she knew when it was breakfast time. She would start off purring and friendly, gently encouraging me to get up and out of bed to give her food. If this failed she did not give up. She would find another way, alter her behaviour in such a way that she provoked the desired response from me. This would include jumping on me, batting my face with her paws, sometimes with her claws out when she was feeling particularly impatient.

It was a very sad day when I realised that I needed to take her to the vets to have her put to sleep. She had started to deteriorate, getting increasingly thin. She completely trusted me as I carried her into the vets room. I stayed with her, stroking her fur and talking gently to her as the vet put her to sleep. Fisher taught me the importance of being independent and never giving up. She also made me realise that death can be a release from pain so it needn't be feared.

If you have animals in your life I am pretty sure that they will teach you valuable lessons too. My dog Ollie is always pleased to see me. It doesn't matter what I look like or what kind of day I have had. As soon as I walk in through the door he bounces up to me, wagging his tail, delighted to see me.

Ollie knows how to show his feelings. He is loyal, happy and full of life. Ollie loves going for walks. I take him out and he is fully focussed, taking in his surroundings. He lives completely in the present, listening to all the sounds, sniffing all the scents and making the most of every moment.

Ollie has taught me how to appreciate my life much more and he reminds me of how fun life is each and every day. He helps me to focus on the things that matter and taking him out every day has put me more in touch with Nature.

Animals live in the Now. They don't spend their days worrying about the future. They don't live their life full of regrets. We truly have a lot to learn from them. You don't need to have a pet yourself to benefit from having them in your life. Why not offer to walk a friend or neighbours dog for them, particularly if they struggle to take them out regularly. That way you have the fun of getting to know an animal without the expense or commitment.

I think it is important that we teach our children to develop a healthy respect for animals. Children need to understand that animals have feelings and needs just as we do. Children that have regular contact with animals tend to feel confident in their presence. Studies suggest that having a cat or dog can help us to reduce stress and feel happier. Patting them and making a fuss of them can really help us to relax.

15. Gurus and Signposting:

I am on a personal development journey. I think it started a number of years ago when I received a book token. I went to the book shop and browsed through the books. One book caught my eye. It was 'The Alchemist' by Paulo Coelho. It is about Santiago, a shepherd boy, who has a recurring dream about a child who tells him that he will find a hidden treasure. The story details his search. I found it very inspiring and I think it is this book that helped me to take the first step on my own journey of self-discovery.

I find that if your mind is open to possibilities then what you learn in one book will prompt you to read another. Sometimes rather than reading books I find watching films equally inspiring.

Another key event in my life was watching the film The Secret by Ronda Byrne who also wrote a book with the same title. It is based on the belief that the power of positive thinking can bring about extraordinary results in your own life. I bought the film and watched it. I was spellbound. I found the people who appeared on it to be fascinating.

Some inspired me more than others so I looked into their work first. Reading one book by one speaker guided me to look into the work of another and so I found The Secret opened many doors for me when the time was right for me to go through them.

I am not saying that you should rush out, buy any particular book or film and follow all the advice that you are given. What I am saying is that when you are willing to listen to new people, you hear new messages explained in ways that could greatly benefit you. I am not suggesting you should blindly follow any or all the advice given by the many life coaches and speakers but I am asking you to keep an open mind and then you can learn from the years of soul searching that other people have experienced. If you are willing to listen to their ideas and guidance you may find that they can help you to improve your life.

Personal development is currently sparking a lot of interest. There are many books, speakers and coaches offering their own approach to attracting health, wealth and happiness. Unfortunately this does mean that some unscrupulous people have realised that there is a lot of money to be made in this area and promises are made that if you sign up to their particular programme you will get rich quick. These promises are quite possibly too good to be true.

I have managed to learn so much from people who have been willing to give up their time on free webinars and who sell their books very cheaply on Kindle. You do not need to spend a fortune buying the latest programme, I have realised. The books and programmes that appeal to you and are affordable by you are likely to be the ones that you will gain most from.

16. Free Webinars:

It is easy to spend a lot of time on The Internet interacting on Facebook and watching entertaining clips on YouTube. I try to establish a time limit on these activities and I keep a look out for educational and inspiring events that are freely offered.

A recent exciting development is the webinar. Webinars are a great way to learn and to interact with like-minded people from around the world. They cut down on the cost, the travel time and the hassle involved with attending seminars. Many of them are live and free. Some encourage interaction with the audience via a phone-in or live web chat.

I have gained a lot from attending them and listening to the guest speakers. As I sign up to one webinar I am often told of other events coming up and am currently on the mailing list of a number of personal development coaches. It can be addictive attending these events as they are generally hosted by upbeat and inspiring people.

I have learnt to be discerning though. Attending too many can be counter-productive. Some hosts offer free webinars mainly to promote their costly products and programmes. This is fair enough if the programmes are of a good quality and the webinar offers useful content in its own right but if the entire event is designed purely to 'plug' a product I am less enthusiastic. The best speakers achieve a good balance between offering a valuable webinar and making people aware of their other products.

You soon learn who these people are and look forward to their events. I am truly appreciative of the inspiring, free content that I have received at times when I have not been in a financial position to purchase services.

17. Inspiring Books:

At times, The Internet is a great way to find new things and to learn about new ideas but at other times books are hard to beat. It does not really matter if you read a real or an e-book, reading is an invaluable way to learn.

I love reading. I can read at my own pace. I can stop and re-read things that really touch me. I read some books through once and never feel the need to re-read them while I feel that other books were written to be read time and time again.

I read a book once and learn something. When I re-read it I notice new things that I had previously missed. I think that this is because as I learn new things this influences my behaviour and experiences so I am approaching things from a new perspective. After I read the work of one author I am eager to learn more about the authors that inspired them.

Inspiring books come in all shapes, sizes and forms. Some are fiction books which offer gripping tales while others are autobiographies where we learn about the individual struggles and achievements of the people we admire. Reading about these experiences makes us realise that we all have joys as well as sorrows. Seeing how people overcome obstacles inspires me to do likewise. Books can be bought very cheaply, on The Internet, in boot-fairs and sales.

Once I have read a book I will consider passing it on to someone who might also benefit from reading it so books can make an inspiring gift too. Some books are too precious to me to give away. I have them displayed proudly on my book shelves and I read them many times. I will buy another copy to give to friends that I feel will benefit from reading them for themselves. Borrowing books from friends or libraries provides us all with great opportunities for learning. It is great fun discussing books that you have shared with your friends.

18. Watch Less TV:

I used to watch a lot of TV. I also never seemed to have much spare time left in the day to do much else. I would come home from work and flop exhausted in front of the TV after cooking dinner. One day I realised that I was spending quite a lot of time watching my favourite shows and that when I watched a lot of TV I often felt more exhausted and irritable than on the days when I didn't. I decided to make a conscious effort to watch less TV once I realised this.

Now I still enjoy relaxing with family and friends in front of the TV but I limit the amount that I watch on a daily basis. All of a sudden I have found that I have a lot more time on my hands and I have started reading, writing and drawing more. Being creative with my spare time has greatly improved the quality of my life. I feel much more alert and I have a lot more energy.

I also try to monitor the kinds of programmes I watch. Comedies are great, they are upbeat and make me laugh and feel happy. I try to avoid programmes that appear overly negative in their content. It is important to know what is happening in the world and I do try to keep myself informed but I avoid watching unproductive slanging matches between politicians, for example. I am willing to watch programmes about people experiencing challenges in their lives providing the possible solutions are also featured. I love watching programmes about people following their dreams and achieving remarkable things.

I believe that it is important to encourage our children to watch less TV and to do something more creative as often as possible. When I look back on my childhood the happy memories are not of being glued to a TV screen but of me out and about enjoying 'The Great Outdoors.' When I ask my own children about their happy memories of growing up, their favourite memories feature being outside too.

Think of your own happy memories. Where were you? I bet you were outdoors a lot of the time.

That said, TV in moderation is fine and can be fun. It can also be very beneficial to watch TV that covers topical issues with your children so that you can discuss what comes up together. This can be very educational and a good way of raising and discussing sensitive issues in a balanced way.

19. Loving Yourself:

It may sound a bit 'fluffy' but the importance of loving yourself should not be underestimated. If you want people to love you, why would they if you don't even like yourself?

Take a good, long, hard look at yourself in the mirror. What do you see? Focus on the things that you like most about your features. I found doing this quite difficult at first but it does get easier with practice. If you struggle to identify anything you do like about your features, pluck up courage and ask a friend or a member of your family what they love about you.

Next you can acknowledge and write down lovable things about you. Yes, I know this can be difficult but you can do it! Once you have a list, pick three things that you love most about your features and three things you love about your character. Look in the mirror and say out loud, "I love you." This may feel very uncomfortable at first but it does get easier. Smile at yourself in the mirror. Think of the things that are lovable about you. You might love your smile, your beautiful eyes and your strong chin. You may love your generosity, your great sense of humour and your ability to cope in a crisis.

If you repeat this exercise often enough you really start to feel happier with yourself. Next time someone offers you a compliment, don't laugh it off, dismiss it or put yourself down. Smile, accept the compliment and add it to the list of things that you love about yourself.

20. EFT Tapping:

When I first heard about Tapping I thought that it sounded weird. I actually dismissed it when I first heard a work colleague mention it as a helpful technique. They told me that they used the technique to release stress and anxiety. I didn't see how tapping yourself could achieve anything of the sort so I instantly dismissed it from my mind. By chance, a year or so later I came across the Tapping World Summit. It was a free event being promoted on the Internet and my curiosity got the better of me and so I decided to sign up. I realised that I had nothing to lose.

EFT stands for Emotional Freedom Technique. Nick Ortner and his sister Jessica were the people that helped me to start to see the benefits of this technique. Basically, you tap on particular areas of your body and this releases stress. These points are called meridian points. First you identify an area of tension within you. You may be feeling a lot of guilt about a recent argument you have had with a loved one, for example.

You could use a 'set up statement' along these lines:

"Even though I am feeling guilty, I love myself anyway."

You restate twice more, "Even though I feel so guilty I love and respect myself now."

"Even though all this guilt is making me feel dreadful, I love every part of me."

You then award your feelings a numerical score out of ten to indicate the severity of your guilt. 0 would indicate no guilt and 10 would indicate extreme guilt. You then tap gently on the series of points as you verbalise your feelings of guilt and this helps to shift your energy and release your feelings.

After you complete a round of Tapping you breathe deeply and reassess your score. It is likely to have reduced. You can carry out more rounds of tapping until your score has dramatically reduced. Once you feel less negative you can complete your Tapping session with positive statements about how much better you feel.

I cannot do full justice to the benefits of Tapping here. If you are at all curious, look into it further, learn from the experts and try it for yourself. I find that Tapping helps relieve me of deep-seated stress and tension. It helps me to be more open to the things that will benefit me. Tapping is used very effectively to help people reduce anxiety, lose weight and is even good for pain relief. I think that Tapping is amazing! Visit the website to find out more for yourself including a demonstration of where and how to tap on the points.

http://www.thetappingsolution.com/

21. Steps to Happiness:

If you are anything like me I expect you find that when things appear to be going well in one area of your life they may seem to be unravelling in another area. We have talked about the importance of achieving a sense of balance in your life.

If you look at each of the areas of your life and you answer these questions honestly you will be able to identify the areas where you can make some changes in order to achieve a healthy balance. Once you have answered all the questions award yourself marks out of 5 for each category. If you score 5/5 in each area it is likely that your life is very happy and fulfilled but many of us fail to achieve such high scores! Pick up to three of your lower scoring areas to work on first.

Answer each question with Yes or No.

Health:
I have a balanced diet and I drink plenty of water.
I get plenty of sleep.
I walk/exercise regularly.
I am free from drug and alcohol addiction.

I am comfortable with the thought of getting older.

Finances:
I am debt free.
My income exceeds my outgoings.
I can afford to have treats and help friends and family financially.
I have a healthy relationship with money.
I know how to economise when I need to.

Home:
I am happy with my home.
I am happy in the area where I live.
I keep my home tidy and clutter-free.
My home is safe.
My home is economical.

Family:
I have/had a good relationship with my parents.
* I have a good relationship with the people I live with.
**I have a good relationship with my children.
I listen to my families needs and they listen to my needs.
We resolve arguments easily.
(* If you live alone and are happy about it then award 1 point.)
(** If you do not have children award 1 point so this does not affect your overall score.)

Friends:
I am happy with my friends.
My friends listen to me and I listen to my friends.
We resolve disagreements amicably.
My friends encourage me to follow my dreams and I encourage my friends.
My friends help me in a crisis and I help my friends in a crisis.

Work:

I have a job I enjoy.

I earn enough money.

I feel secure and appreciated in my job.

I have a good work/life balance.

I enjoy working with the people I work with.

Relaxation:

I have a hobby/interest that I enjoy.

I set aside time to relax.

My family/friends support my interests.

I spend some time alone and some with family and friends.

I have enough time free for my interests.

Spirituality and Beliefs:

I respect the beliefs of others and other people respect my beliefs.

I have tried meditation.

I appreciate the beauty of Nature.

I do not fear death.

My friends respect my beliefs and I respect my friend's beliefs.

Emotional Health:

I express my feelings and am aware of the feelings of others.

I love myself.

I feel loved by others.

I am not ashamed to cry.

I am not afraid to ask my friends/family for help if I need it.

Award yourself 1 point for every 'Yes' answer.

Once you have responded to these questions total up the points. Look carefully at the areas where you have scored the least points. These are the areas to work on first. It is good to have two goals to work on. One that seems relatively easy to achieve and another that may require more effort. Picking an easy to achieve goal is sensible as you can quickly and easily reap the benefits of your efforts which is likely to motivate you to achieve the more difficult goal.

This book does not detail how to set and achieve your goals, it is intended as a springboard to get you started. There are plenty of books and CD's on the market that can help you to set and achieve goals. I would urge you to act to achieve balance in your life. This has enormous benefits to you and to the people around you.

In addition to books and CD's there are coaches, charities and health organisations that can help you improve many areas of your life. It can be hard to take the decision to make changes in your life. Remember every little step in the right direction is beneficial. Set goals with easily achievable steps that you can measure and feel the benefits as you move closer to achieving your main goals.

Each area of your life is important so try not to neglect any area. It is helpful to repeat the questionnaire above from time to time to see if there are any other areas of your life that have fallen out of balance. I find that when I make positive changes in one area of my life this brings about unexpected benefits in other areas. Try it for yourself and see if it works for you.

22. Laughter:

Laughing is so beneficial to your health. Shared jokes can bring people together and Comedy can be used to break down barriers between people. Few people can avoid smiling when they hear babies chuckle!

Life can be stressful and it can be easy to feel rather worn down at times. If you do feel life has been dragging you down lately, take time to make a list of the things that make you smile. If there are people in your life who are often able to cheer you up, go and visit them. See what comedies are being released and go and see them at the cinema. Don't worry if you have nobody to go with. I have been to the cinema alone many times and find it to be a great experience. If you cannot afford the cinema prices, a cheaper alternative would be to visit charity shops and look for inexpensive comedy DVD's and have a fun night in watching them. Why not invite a friend to join you?

Laughing can even speed up your recovery when you are ill. The only problem is when you have had an operation requiring abdominal stitches and someone makes you laugh, that is agony!

Seeing the funny side can have the benefit of defusing conflicts.

At times I have been in the middle of a heated argument with my daughter when something funny happens and we both burst out laughing, the air has been cleared and the argument suddenly forgotten.

Smiling really lights up people's faces. Laughter is infectious. Next time you are out walking or even standing in a queue, make eye-contact with someone and smile at them. They will nearly always smile back. If someone smiles at me in the street it instantly lights up my life and can make the world seem a better place for a little while at least.

23. Negative Thoughts and Anxiety:

One negative thought left unchecked can lead to another and then another. You can soon feel bogged down by all the negativity that surrounds you. It reminds me of the poem:

'For the Want of a Horse Shoe Nail.' Benjamin Franklin
"For the want of a nail the shoe was lost,
For the want of a shoe the horse was lost,
For the want of a horse the rider was lost,
For the want of a rider the battle was lost,
For the want of the battle the war was lost,
For the want of the war the kingdom was lost,
And all for the want of a horse shoe nail."

In my life when I start to think negatively this soon escalates and leads to one of those awful days when everything seems to go wrong. We have all had them haven't we? Now I do still think negatively but when I catch myself doing this I take time to listen carefully to my negative self-talk and decide if I need to take any action to improve the situation.

If there is an action I can take to improve things then I will act but usually the talk is all about things that have gone wrong in the past or may possibly happen in the future. I realise that this stems out of a wish for self-preservation. I think it is a mistaken belief that if I expect and prepare for the worst case scenario I will be shielded from hurt if disaster strikes. In reality, thinking this way erodes my confidence and doesn't help me to prepare for mishaps at all. When I catch myself thinking negatively I silently thank my subconscious mind for trying to keep me safe but also firmly remind myself that these thoughts are not serving me so I gently release them.

I find EFT Tapping can help release negative thoughts when they occur. I used to bury and suppress negative thoughts but soon discovered that this doesn't work either. Suppressing layer upon layer of negative thoughts can lead to anxiety and depression. I try to look for the most positive outcome in any given situation and usually I succeed but just like everyone I have my challenges and days where negative thoughts prevail. On those days when I realise how I am feeling I am kind to myself and remind myself that I am doing the best that I can at that particular time.

24. Symbols in Nature:

Some people believe in angels. They say that they live among us, guarding and keeping us safe and that they are here to assist us whenever we ask for help. Whether you believe in them or not, it doesn't really matter. Angels do exist in some religions and are portrayed by artists in beautiful paintings so at least we have some awareness of what they might look like. Some people even believe that good people are angels in human form while others imagine them as celestial beings complete with halo's and wings.

Because angels are said to have wings, when a feather is found lying on the ground this can be regarded as a sign that the angels are watching over you nearby. I rather like this idea. Whenever I find a pretty feather I smile and take it as a sign that everything is right with the world.

Another beautiful symbol from nature is a rainbow. The colours are lovely and they occur at times when we experience both sunshine and showers. Christians take the rainbow as a reminder that God has promised never to send another flood as devastating as that experienced when Noah build his ark. Whether you are Christian or not, the rainbow appears at times of sunshine and showers and reminds us in our darkest moments that sunnier times lie just around the corner.

I love rainbows. I am always excited when I see them. To me, they symbolise hope and promise. If you see a rainbow when you are in an aeroplane, flying above the clouds, you see a perfect circle rather than an arc. I find that amazing. Science has an explanation for rainbows that involves light and refraction. Apparently we all see our own individual rainbow. When you think about that it does make the rainbow seem even more special.

There are so many other things in nature that we can take as positive symbols.

The butterfly signifies new life and transformation, for example. Finding pretty worn down glass pebbles on the beach reminds me that often beauty comes with age.

If you find a conch shell and put it to your ear it is said that you can hear the secrets told by the sea. Natural objects can really help to keep us in touch with what really matters in life, particularly now in our fast-paced age of technology.

'Butterflies are symbols of transformation.'

25. Friendship:

Friends are so important. At key points in my life I have made good and lasting friendships. When I was a teenager at school, I made friends with some people that I am still in touch with. When my children were born I made more friends who still remain a big part of my life.

Friends are likely to have things in common with you and are often less likely to judge you than some members of your family. Some people have few family members that they relate to but enjoy a strong friendship network. Some friendships are life-long. They stand the test of time. They develop and grow over time while other friendships can be intense to start with but they soon fade.

In life we change and move in new directions. This is not a bad thing. At these times we sometimes lose touch with some friends while making new ones. Some friends can adapt and adjust as we change, while others cannot or will not.

It took me a long time to realise that short term friendships and acquaintances can be good too. You meet someone, you enjoy their company, you spend time together but then circumstances change and you start to drift apart. I now realise that although this type of friendship comes and then goes, these friendships are still well worth having.

Good friends sometimes let you know when you have made a mistake. They find a kind way of letting you know when they they feel you have come unstuck in some way. They listen to you when you need a shoulder to cry on and when they need you then you are there for them too.

Friendships can test you and this can help you to grow stronger. Sometimes we make mistakes and ask for forgiveness and at other times friends let us down and we learn how to forgive them. Having a good friend can teach you a lot about yourself and can help you to become more caring and loving towards others.

26. NLP
Neuro Linguistic Programming:

I am relatively new to NLP. It is a useful way to help people make positive changes in their lives. When you go to see a practitioner they will ask you what you want out of life. They will ask you how achieving your target would make you feel and they will offer you helpful techniques and resources to enable you to vividly imagine yourself achieving your goals. They will help you identify any resources you currently have that will help you achieve your goals and they will also enable you to approach life differently to allow the things that you currently lack to enter your life. NLP practitioners encourage you to make full use of your senses in order to bring about change.

Let's imagine you have contacted an NLP practitioner for help with giving up smoking. They will ask you to picture vividly what life would be like for you when you have achieved your goal. They will ask you to describe what you would look like, what people would say to you. They will ask you to state how you would smell when you are smoke-free, how things will taste and how your skin will feel. The techniques that they use can help you to bring about rapid change in your life. People have used NLP to help them reduce anxiety and fear. People have also received help achieving dating confidence, public speaking confidence and they have received help with overcoming job interview nerves. NLP can also help with weight loss.

I have undertaken NLP training and am benefiting from putting the techniques that I learn into practice in my own life. I am also very willing to help others using these techniques if they would like me to.

We are lucky enough to be living in exciting times where a whole range of techniques are being developed that can really help us to cope and thrive in our sometimes confusing, often fast-paced modern lives. With any coaching it is important that you work with someone you can relate to and who treats you with courtesy and respect. Take time to read testimonials and ask for a taster session to help you decide if the coach is right for you. I would definitely recommend that you try NLP for yourself as it really can help.

27. Self-hypnosis:

I always used to be a little suspicious of hypnosis. I am usually an open-minded person but for some reason the prospect of a hypnotist putting me into a trance made me feel somewhat threatened. It would be a terrible thing to be put into a trance, lose control and make a fool of myself. I think this is because essentially I am quite a private person and like to keep my inner-most thoughts to myself. It doesn't help that stage hypnosis has become quite popular. This is where the hypnotist is up on stage and chooses his or her 'victim' from the audience. They are summoned up onto the stage. Once up there the volunteer is put into a state of deep hypnosis. In some cases it is claimed that the victims are encouraged to strip off their clothes or pretend to be a chicken. Having this happen to me would be amongst my worst nightmares.

I have recently reviewed my attitude to hypnosis as I have undertaken a course in self-hypnosis. Hypnotist Ed Leicester offers a modular course. Each module offers a guided hypnosis. You are asked to travel in your mind to exciting places in order to unlock your dreams. The aim is that during the process, you find the characteristics needed to achieve your dreams. I came across this on-line course by accident. I decided to challenge myself to try something I had little belief in to see if it would impact on me in any way. I decided to reserve my judgement, completed each module and discovered that hypnosis can really help you to discover what you want to achieve in life as well as give you the self confidence needed to achieve your goals.

I have also learnt that nobody can hypnotise you against your will and nobody can make you do anything that you are unhappy with. Interestingly, we actually spend a lot of time in a hypnotic state. As we daydream we transport ourselves into the past and the future which means that in our minds we regularly move through space and time as we think of past times and future possible events.

28. Feng Shui:

I have just started learning about Feng Shui. It is an area that is starting to hold some fascination for me. I have always been a bit of a hoarder and as my children grew up I stored many of their cute little clothes and toys as they outgrew them, along with pictures they produced and photos we had taken.

While I still believe it would be a shame to throw it all away, a few months ago I started to look around my house and realised that it was filled with things that I had not looked at in years and I am unlikely to need in the future.

If you move house regularly it is quite likely that you will de-clutter each time you move which serves to keep your possessions under control. If, like me, on the other hand you have lived in the same place for a number of years it is more likely that your possessions will have 'stacked up.'

Until recently I told myself that it didn't really matter if I had a few things piled up here and there but now I have started to realise that living surrounded by clutter muddles my mind and saps my motivation to get things done. I planned to move house and so I had a perfect incentive to do something about it. I spent a few weeks cleaning out my house and I sold or gave away any unwanted items such as the DVD's that I no longer watched, as well as CD's that I no longer listened to. I sold items at boot-fairs, gave things away to charity shops and took the real rubbish down to the local tip. Surplus papers were shredded and recycled.

I found this a very difficult process trying to decide what I no longer needed and it was hard to be sure of what I was ready to part with but I had a good incentive. I knew that I intended downsizing and moving to a much smaller dwelling and any excess stuff would really get in the way.

I have to admit that now that I have moved and am living in a small cosy caravan I feel a lot better having gone through this house clearing process. Now I am able to live a lot more simply. I have started to look into Feng Shui now that I can see the benefits of de-cluttering my surroundings.

The way items are placed and even the materials that they are made from can influence the atmosphere of your home. Having a jungle of over-grown plants by the entrance of your home can send out unwelcoming signals, for example. Dirty windows stops light entering your home and can lead to you feeling stuck and depressed. I am definitely starting to open my mind to what Feng Shui can teach me. Why don't you look into it too?

29. Healthy Eating:

You are what you eat. It is as simple as that. If you are eating a lot of processed fast-food you could well be eating too much salt, sugar and artificial additives. In the long term this could lead to health problems. If you eat a lot of cheap meat that has been produced in intensive farms then the quality of the meat is unlikely to be very good. The lives led by these animals, prior to slaughter will be far from ideal too.

Organic meat and vegetables can be more expensive but are more nutritious.

If you are able to rear the animals humanely yourself and grow your own fruit and vegetables the taste is likely to be better, far better. If you can't rear your own animals and grow your own vegetables then buying locally from small ethical farms is a fantastic way to support your local community as well as ensuring the animals have been treated fairly.

Learning how to cook a few basic, nutritious meals from scratch using good quality ingredients is an excellent way of safeguarding your health and that of your family. Teaching children to cook is a really important life skill. This will help them when they leave home and look after themselves. If they can cook for themselves they are likely to be able to eat well and save money.

If I do eat out I prefer to go to restaurants where they use a few basic ingredients and keep the food wholesome and simple. I am disappointed when I eat out to find microwaved fast-food served up as home made food. Eating healthy food is enjoyable. It tastes delicious.

If you start by growing your own tomatoes and then serve them in a simple salad, I am sure you will taste the difference and this will spur you on to grow more things for yourself. You don't need a lot of garden space to do this and some vegetables can be grown in tubs.

30. Exercise:

I think we all know that exercise is important if we are to remain fit and healthy. For people to keep exercising they need to find a form of exercise that they are happy with. Not everybody enjoys going to the gym, for example. Some people go for their initial assessment, sign up in January for a year and by February they have quit. If going to the gym does not appeal to you there are many alternatives.

Some people enjoy dancing, others like tennis or squash. Personally, I enjoy walking and particularly enjoy walking my dog. I got my dog 5 years ago and I never fail to take him out for a walk at least twice a day. Walking a dog can be excellent exercise and good for your social life. When I am out walking my dog many more people talk to me, particularly fellow dog owners. If you don't have a dog then maybe a friend or neighbour has one that you can walk. They might really appreciate you offering to take their dog out, particularly if they find it hard to get out and about themselves. Another great thing about dog walking is that it is free!

Swimming is an excellent form of exercise, particularly if you have a back injury as the water can support you as you exercise. Obviously if you are being treated for an injury, seek medical advice before taking any form of exercise to ensure you do not damage yourself further. Most public swimming baths offer lessons to non-swimmers so don't let an inability to swim or a fear of the water put you off.

There are many other excellent forms of exercise including Yoga and Pilates. These are popular for strengthening and toning your muscles as well as relieving stress. Martial arts offer excellent forms of exercise and many classes are offered. This has the added benefit of providing you with useful self defence techniques.

If you are unfit and have not exercised for years it can be daunting to break the habits of a lifetime but even a little regular exercise can increase your fitness and improve your health. Some people prefer exercising alone while others are more motivated by a group. Some exercise can cost money while other forms are completely free. Find whatever works for you and get started. The benefits of exercise are enormous and the consequences of being unfit can be potentially serious.

31. Go For No!

If you really want to achieve something, you can. Let's say you are an artist and you want to sell your work, what is to stop you painting a picture then taking it down to a gallery and asking the owner to include the work in their next show? For many of us it is the fear of our work being rejected that holds us back. Whether you are a potential musician, author or salesperson, the real barrier to progress is the fear of someone telling us we are not good or just simply telling us 'No.' If you have a good project or idea that you truly believe in then don't stop yourself from offering your product or service to others.

I came across an approach on The Internet by Andrea Waltz. It is called 'Go For No.' There is also a book. I found it extremely useful. The theory is that if you have a good product and you offer it to enough people after a significant number of rejections some people will immediately say yes to your product and others may say 'No for Now' but may approach you later when the situation changes and they have need for your product. This is described as failing your way to being successful. It is not uncommon for 8 out of 10 people to say no to a good product and so you may be rejected many times before someone says yes. The key is not to give up. Successful people are regularly rejected but they never give up.

J.K Rowling, the author of Harry Potter and world famous pop band The Beatles were originally rejected and had they given up then they would never have gone on to enjoy their later success. Have belief in yourself and Go For No. This could really change your life.

Find out more at: www.**goforno**.com

32. Follow Your Path:

As we grow up we listen to the influential people in our lives and they have a tendency to guide us towards an occupation that they feel we would be well suited to. This is probably well intended but it may not turn out to be what really is right for us.

When I was young, people believed a sensible career to aim for would be to work in a bank. The hours were good and at the time it was thought to provide a 'job for life.' Many caring parents encouraged their children to work in this field and many of their children followed their advice. Quite a number of those same individuals were made redundant during the economic downturn and were left wondering where they had gone wrong. I am not saying that working in a bank is the wrong thing to do if it is something that interests you. People who are good with figures and are well suited to Customer Service could flourish in this role but it isn't for everyone.

A friend of mine was about to go to Law School but really wanted to become a musician. They told me this only days before they went to Law School. Their family had advised them to get a 'good, solid profession' behind them and so they did. Years later they left the Law profession but they never did pursue their musical career. I always wondered if life would have been different if they had followed their dreams.

I believe that children should be encouraged to follow their dreams. I am not saying it has to be 'all or nothing.' Some people manage to work a day job and find enough time and energy to pursue their passion as a hobby and other people manage to juggle two careers. I believe that a parent's role is to support and encourage their children to decide for themselves what is right for them. We are generally good at what we enjoy doing and so if we work at what we love we are more likely to be successful than if we turn up to do something 5 or more days a week that we really do not enjoy. My advice would be this: If you are good at doing something that you love doing and you think you may be able to make a living doing it, don't you owe it to yourself to give it a try?

Caption *'Follow your path.'*

33. Goal Setting:

Are there things that you would like to achieve in your life? Would you like to go on a particular holiday or would you like to own a new car, perhaps? You may have a whole list of things that you would like to achieve.

One effective way to step closer to your dreams is to set yourself goals. Let's imagine that you have always wanted to visit India, well, what is stopping you going? It may be lack of money, lack of time or a fear of flying. Start by identifying and writing down all the things that are getting in the way of you achieving your dream. Look at the barriers carefully and decide which ones are easiest to remove. It may be that you have no passport. This should be relatively simple to remedy. Go and pick up an application form, fill it in and you are on your way. Sending off for your passport may feel like a small but significant step towards achieving your goal.

Next you can decide where you would like to go. Be specific. Where would you like to go and for how long? How would you like to get there and when would you like to go? Browse through brochures to find exactly where you would like to stay and research fights etc. Make a detailed list of places and prices and then you have a much clearer idea of what funds you will require in order to make your dream a reality. Look into visa's, vaccines, everything you need to organise, if you are to make this trip.

Work out an accurate cost for your trip. Once you have a figure, try not to feel daunted. There are all sorts of imaginative ways to raise the cash. You may even win it in a competition. It is all about being open to possibilities and acting on opportunities when they present themselves to you. You can sell unwanted items, freeing up space around you as well as raising some money. You can ask your friends and family to give you travel vouchers for Christmas and birthday gifts. By sharing your goal with others this helps you to focus on your goal and it makes it feel real. Saving your spare change in a jar then banking it and saving money by switching energy suppliers are just two more ways of stepping closer to your goal.

Life has a curious way of rewarding people who take regular action. If you remain focussed on your goals and stay open to the opportunities that present themselves to you, then you will be able to take steps that will bring you closer to achieving your dreams.

34. Keeping a Journal or Diary:

Have you ever kept a journal or a diary? This is an excellent way to express and record your thoughts and feelings. You can look back over previous diary entries in order to see how you have grown and developed over the years. You can look at recent entries and if they seem overly negative this can help you to recognise areas that you may choose to change in your life next.

Diaries can become a valuable wake-up call. If you read back over entry after entry and you seem to be repeating experiences, this may be a sign that you need to change the way you approach things in order to achieve more positive outcomes.

Another benefit from recording your thoughts in a diary is that you can begin to turn your thoughts into something more concrete. Scribbling down any ideas that pop into your head can be a great way of deciding on which action steps you can take next. Writing down your dreams and wishes can help you to formulate plans and actions that are needed in order to turn your dreams into reality. All the best inventions were created when a spark of an idea occurred in someone's head and they were inspired to take action. If inventors hadn't acted on their original idea it may have been lost and forgotten.

A diary is an excellent way to record the progress you are making in your life, including any attempts made to change unhealthy behaviour, such as drinking too much. Diary entries can be used as a basis for a novel. Your life is unique and recording the story of your life could be the first step towards producing a book that could appeal to others. Recording the ups and downs of life in a diary, looking back over the happy and sad times, recording any poignant moments can really help to get the juices flowing for a future novel.

I really enjoy keeping a diary. It helps me to reduce any feelings of stress that I may be experiencing. By writing my hopes and fears down, I no longer have them 'bottled up' inside me. I can act upon good ideas and let my less productive thoughts go. Plenty of famous people have kept a diary and the world would be a considerably less rich place without their contribution.

35. Art:

I find drawing and painting very therapeutic. We aren't all Michelangelo but we don't need to be. There is only one Michelangelo and there is only one you. You are unique. Drawing and painting takes many different forms. Some paintings are abstract and other artists paint in a more realistic style. Using different mediums affects the end result too. You do not need to spend a lot of money buying expensive equipment. You can transform a doodle scribbled onto an envelope with pen into a work of art. A cheap set of watercolours can be very effectively used or you can draw with a simple pencil. If you feel totally daunted at the prospect of 'going it alone' why not enrol in a drawing or painting class? Many classes are inexpensive and take place near you.

Even choosing interesting pictures from magazines, cutting them out and arranging them can create a very attractive collage. Some people enjoy finding a photo of an interesting face. They cut it in half, stick one half onto the paper and then draw in the other half. This is a very effective way of developing our drawing talents.

Charcoals and pastels are great fun to use. You can blur the edges you draw and create stunning effects. Creating a still-life using everyday objects is also great fun. Experimenting with different types of paint such as oil or acrylic can be exciting too. Local discount shops often sell paint and other art products cheaply. Why not go and see what you can find?

So many people were put off art when they were told by someone in their past that they were no good at drawing. If a young child is told that they are not good at art by a parent or teacher then this is likely to crush their creative spirit and the truth is we are all artists and very capable of creating our own original pieces. Why not give it a try?

36. Music:

Music is inspiring. It is also freely available to us. If you go to a boot-fair or table sale, people are virtually giving away CD's that they no longer listen to. There are sites on The Internet such as You Tube where you can listen to music and watch videos.

We all have our favourite musicians and it can be wonderful to watch them Live at concerts and music festivals. It can be great fun to watch a local band playing at the pub down the road. There are often local bands and musicians playing in pubs and admission is usually free. Why not learn to play a musical instrument yourself? My son started off by teaching himself how to play a cheap keyboard and now he is at university studying music.

Singing is completely free. Singing along to your favourite songs while driving to work or while relaxing in the bath is very enjoyable. These are two of my favourite occupations. Music is an excellent way to inspire and inform others. Many musicians are able to express their ideas to others through the medium of music. Almost everyone finds music accessible.

At different points in my life, lyrics from certain songs really start to resonate with me. When I hear a musician put my feelings into words I am very touched. Certain songs strike a chord with many of us and this makes a real difference to our lives.

There are so many different music genres and each offers us something different. World Music is wonderful. In every country there are traditional musicians who have learnt their craft from Master musicians. Music transcends all ages and is accessible throughout the world.

Children love making and decorating their own musical instruments. They usually love singing unless they are told by a teacher or family member that they can't sing. The truth is we can all sing and so let's celebrate this!

37. Subconscious Abundance Blocks:

Do you ever set yourself a goal and then struggle to achieve it?

Let's imagine that you are trying to lose weight. You start off enthusiastically planning out a diet and exercise regime, you buy healthy food and you get started. Things go well at first. You lose a few pounds and you feel proud of yourself but then you weigh yourself a week later and find that not only have you failed to lose any more weight you have even put some weight back on again! This is so de-motivating that you give up, go to the cupboard, find some biscuits and you 'scoff the lot.' You have officially given up the weight loss campaign and you tell yourself that you don't care that you have not lost weight, that dieting is pointless and you carry on with your life.

This kind of thing happens to all of us at some point in our lives. There are all kinds of reasons why this occurs but one reason for our failure is that we develop self-limiting beliefs. We adopt negative self-talk that blocks our chances of success. One part of us really wants to lose weight and plans the diet, while another part is convinced that we won't be able to achieve our goal and so sabotages our efforts. Our subconscious mind runs a commentary of self-talk that is not always positive and if this talk contradicts our goal then we are unlikely to achieve it. This self-talk is intended to keep us safe. It stops us from taking risks and potentially getting hurt. We remind ourselves of any previous attempts to achieve our goals that have failed. This reminder can stop us being willing to risk trying again in future.

Subconscious blocks can be removed once we are aware of them. One effective way of doing this is by quietly listening to the chatter in your head and when you notice negative talk, gently release it as it no longer serves you. You can also use EFT Tapping to help release all this anxiety and fear.

38. Downsizing:

My children have grown up and left home to go to University. This means that I no longer need a three bedroom house and a few months ago I decided that it was time for me to downsize. I put my house on the market and once it sold I bought a residential caravan. Downsizing isn't right for everyone but I believe it is right for me.

I slowly cleared out all my surplus possessions. Items I no longer needed were sold at boot fairs, some were donated to Charity shops and any junk was recycled. I have found this to be a very positive process although it was very difficult to decide on what to give away and what to keep. My house became clearer than it has ever been and I am determined not to cram too many possessions into my smaller space now that I have moved. A lot of people are deciding to downsize and live a simpler life, to cut down on outgoings and save money for their retirement. The cost of living is high and for many, wages are not keeping up.

Downsizing appears to be a simple solution to this problem and it also appeals to people who wish to reduce their working hours as they get older. Work can be a very important, rewarding part of life but it is important to achieve a balance between work and play in life. Downsizing can mean that we can afford to work less hours and achieve a better work/life balance.

39. Dream Job:

We spend a lot of our time at work. We need to earn enough money to live and to support our families. Some people feel stuck in a rut at work and are looking for alternative ways to earn money. Other people have been unable to find work and feel under incredible pressure to find employment.

I have been lucky enough to enjoy my work over the years and when I have decided to move on I have been always able to find interesting new opportunities. As we spend such a long time working, I believe that it is important that we find our occupation rewarding.

Look around you and you will find people's attitude to work varies enormously. In the Supermarket I always queue at a checkout where staff appear happy in their work. I also return to restaurants where the staff are enthusiastic and friendly.

If you do not enjoy your job, it may be time to consider applying for a new role. Other people may enjoy a job that you would hate so leaving a job you loathe leaves it open for someone who would find it rewarding. In times of high unemployment the thought of changing jobs can be daunting but if you keep an open mind and are determined to make changes, there are a whole range of opportunities out there for you.

You can scan the Situations Vacant where you may find your dream job or you could identify somewhere that you would like to work even if there is no job advertised. You could offer your services by calling in to meet the staff and hand in your CV. I have heard of a surprising number of people who have created jobs for themselves in this way.

You could consider setting up your own business. If you have a skill or service to offer this could be a positive step forward for you. It may be that you are a good photographer and will find your skills in demand once other people know about you. You could start working part-time and increase your hours once you become established. You could consider a career in Multi Level Marketing which can be an exciting way of making a living and provides you with a residual income. Developing a creative approach to finding a job can open the door to new possibilities.

40. Doing What You Love:

It is possible to serve others by doing the things you love.

If you are passionate about what you do you will do it well and people are likely to wish to work with you.

I recently watched a TV programme where a couple who were approaching retirement, decided to establish their own business together doing something they both enjoy. They bought an ancient camper van, lovingly restored it and turned it into a beautiful travelling vintage tea room. They took their van to festivals and served delicious cream teas. I believe this venture was so successful because of the passion that they both had for the project. Their enthusiasm was infectious!

It doesn't matter what your hobbies and interests are. If you enjoy your hobby enough you could turn this into an employment opportunity for yourself. If you are a good artist why not exhibit and sell your work? If you are a good listener you could consider becoming a coach or a counsellor.

If you enjoy making clothes you could make a living selling your creations. It may well be that your business will be part-time at first and then when it establishes itself well, you could consider building it into a full time occupation. You will not know if your business could work out unless you give it a try.

I firmly believe that doing what we love is how we are meant to live. Somewhere along the line we were convinced that our job has to be hard work and we only get to have fun in our spare time. Where did we get this idea from?

I realise that we need to earn enough money to pay our bills and successfully run our lives but I sometimes fear that many of us have given up all hope of living a happy life. Look carefully at your life. If your job is not making you happy, examine your options. Finding a new job or starting a new business could well be the answer. This also applies if you do not currently have a job and you are seeking work. Try applying for jobs that you think you would enjoy, you never know if you will be successful unless you try.

41. Habits:

Our habits tend to rule our lives.

Establishing positive habits can make such a difference to your life. When we look around us we realise that our habits contribute to where we are in life. If we are overweight, we may have failed to establish a healthy eating habit and an exercise habit. We may have decided that we want to lose weight but we cannot make changes using willpower alone.

Our subconscious habits establish themselves over time and can be very hard to break. If we do decide that we wish to make changes in our lives, it is important to be aware of certain habits that may influence our goals. We need to start by truthfully appraising the current situation. How did we get to be the way we are now?

If we are overweight and wish to lose weight, how did we become overweight in the first place and how is this serving us? It may be that as small children we were upset and our parents gave us sweets to cheer us up. In this case we form a positive association with eating sweets so whenever we feel upset we eat sweets to cheer ourselves up and this can lead to us putting on weight.

The eating of sweets serves to comfort us so even though this habit is not entirely healthy it does benefit us in some way. In this example, recognising how we became overweight and how the over-eating has served us we can begin to find healthier ways to cheer ourselves up when we feel sad, thus replacing the old habit with a healthier new one.

It is good to vividly imagine how we would feel if we reached a healthier weight. How would we look? What would people say to us? We can use our senses to really imagine how we would be. We could imagine ourselves eating healthy food that we enjoy and set ourselves small achievable steps towards our achieving our goal. Making positive affirmations and rewarding ourselves with small non-food orientated treats can really help us to change our habits.

When we take a step backwards it is important not to feel a failure. We can still treat ourselves kindly, remind ourselves that all is not lost and simply continue to take steps towards changing our habits for the better as soon as we feel able to. Once a healthy eating habit is firmly established then the benefits of living in this new way will begin to be recognised and absorbed by the subconscious. It will start to work with us rather than against us.

42. Family:

Families can be a source of happiness but sometimes they can be a source of stress. Some people have a large, close family and others have very little contact with theirs. Family relationships can have their ups and downs and this can affect your life in many ways. Some people feel very loved and supported by their family while others feel stifled by their family relationships. Your relationship with your family is unique to you. You may be very happy with your current situation or you may wish to make changes.

Communication is often the key to positive family relationships. Being able to listen carefully to your family as well as feeling able to express your feelings effectively helps to establish family harmony. Certain experiences can put a strain on family relationships. If one family member does something which is outside of the family norm this can create tension. Some families struggle when an unmarried member of their family becomes pregnant, for example.

As individuals, we aim to be happy while remaining on good terms with our family. Sometimes this can be difficult to achieve. Balancing individual wishes against family obligation can be a challenge. This is more likely to achieved where there is give and take demonstrated by all parties.

The structure of The Family varies greatly too. Some people live with their extended family while other people live with one parent. Some families are regarded as traditional in their values, while others adopt a less conventional approach. Providing attempts are made to meet the needs of all family members the family bond is likely to remain strong and positive. If you and your family are happy with your lives, does it really matter what the rest of society thinks?

I believe that so long as you are not hurting others you should be free to live the life you love and to me family is at its best when it supports and encourages family members to follow their dreams.

43. Active Listening:

Active listening is hard. At least I find it hard.

A friend starts talking, I start off by listening to them but as they continue speaking my mind starts to formulate a response to what they are saying even before they have finished. I cease to listen so carefully. I used to have a tendency to butt-in and add what I thought was a relevant comment here and there but I have learnt to hold back from doing this. I am currently working on fully listening to what people say before I start to think of a response. Often when people are speaking they are not looking for advice, they are really wanting someone to listen to them carefully.

Active listening also involves observing someone's body language. They may well be saying one thing but their body language may be revealing that they are really thinking and feeling something different. An example of this might be when someone says that they are really looking forward to going to a party but their closed body language and unenthusiastic facial expression may betray their true feelings on the matter.

I have started to realise that active listening involves being 'interested not interesting.' By this I mean focussing on what someone is saying is more important that trying to cultivate a witty response at the expense of concentrating on what is actually being said. Listening carefully to people can really improve the quality of your interactions with them. If you truly listen to someone, they are much more likely to make the effort to listen to you. Try this yourself. The more you listen to people the more you are listened to. As our communication becomes more effective we feel more respected, valued and appreciated by those around us.

44. Failure:

It is said that there is no such thing as failure, only feedback. This can be hard to accept.

It took me a long time to pass my driving test. The first two attempts were unsuccessful, I was 20. I decided that driving wasn't important to me at the time. Public transport was fairly reliable where I lived and at the time I didn't feel the need to own a car so I stopped trying to drive. Even when I had my children, not being able to drive wasn't a real hardship to me. I actually enjoyed walking the children to school and I didn't mind taking the train to go on holiday but once I became a teacher I was often required to travel as part of my job. I had to attend training courses in inaccessible places and I started to realise that not being able to drive was starting to become a real setback for me. I decided that I would try and pass my driving test.

I didn't have much confidence in my ability at the time but I booked some lessons and to my amazement I slowly made progress. I re-took my test 20 years after the last failure. I was so nervous that I failed again. I re-took the test a further 4 times before I finally passed! The day I passed my test I felt wonderful. All the lessons and test failures actually built up my confidence and provided me with the driving experiences I needed to have in order to pass. I firmly believe that all these experiences combined to make me a safer driver.

The key point that I am making here is that if you believe in yourself enough you will get there in the end. Many famous and successful people did not get what they wanted the first time they tried.

This proverb is so useful: 'If at first you don't succeed, try, try, try again.'

Obviously you do need to be willing to learn from your experiences. If, for example, you apply for a job and attend an interview and you are not offered the job, try and pluck up courage to ask for feedback. Listen to what is said to you and if the feedback offered is constructive then act on what you are being told. Most people are willing to offer feedback to people who genuinely want to improve. If you are brave enough to listen and then act on any useful suggestions that are made, you are much more likely to succeed next time you apply for a similar job. If something doesn't come that easily to you but you keep working on it, when you finally succeed you will feel incredible!

45. Inspiring Quotes:

Sometimes someone says something to you that really strikes a chord within you. When this happens to me I usually try and write the quote down. I have a number of notebooks containing quotes that have provided me with inspiration throughout my life.

Words mean different things to each person and what touches you now may have less impact at a later stage in your life. Words are very powerful. What you say has the power to crush or inspire. I try to remember this and give thought to what I am saying so I am more likely to uplift people than discourage them.

Confucius said: "It doesn't matter how slow you go as long as you do not stop."

I think this is true. There are days when we struggle to motivate ourselves. If we can manage to achieve one small thing at these times we are likely to arrive at our chosen destination. On Facebook I do share quotes that uplift and inspire me in the hope that they may also inspire others. I write down quotes that particularly move me. Sometimes I write down the lyrics from a song. Song words really can lift and move people.

46. Social Networking:

Technology has moved on in recent years and social networking sites come and go, bringing people a mix of joys and sorrows. Used carefully, I find these sites are a good way of staying in touch with friends and for contacting like-minded people.

The first social networking site I used was My-Space. My daughter helped me to set up my profile and I began to explore what the site had to offer. I loved the Writer's Forum. It was a space where people who loved creative writing could share their talent and enthusiasm for the written word. We used to write short stories and poems and share them with one another so people could critique our work. Sadly My-Space closed the forum's so I decided that it was time to explore Facebook. I created a profile and started accepting friends and soon afterwards I discovered the merits of Twitter and created a Twitter profile too.

With any social networking site it is important that you keep yourself safe and respect the privacy of others. Anything you write can be seen by a potentially huge audience. There are a range of security settings that you can use to protect yourself. Using a public setting means that literally anyone can see what you post so if you choose this setting think carefully about what you decide to post. I try not to overuse the sites as they can be addictive. I love the inspirational quotes and pictures that are posted and I like helping other people to celebrate their birthday by posting on their wall.

The down side to social networking is that some people are obsessed by appearances and so only put the very best photo's of themselves up. This can give the site an unrealistic, rosy tinted image and some people can feel inadequate when they compare themselves to others. It is good to ensure we don't spend so long social networking that real life passes us by. It is great to share our joys and sorrows with our friends and family but it is important to spend more time actually living life than posting about it.

47. Blogging:

I have a blog. A blog is a bit like a diary. It is produced and then published online. A blog can be posted onto social networking sites such as Facebook so that friends and family can easily access it.

Why keep a blog?

For me, writing a blog is like keeping a diary but with one key difference. A blog is potentially public, while many of us elect to keep what we write in our diaries secret. I find keeping a blog helps me to keep a record of what is going on in my life but knowing that people potentially read what I write helps me to ensure that I keep the content positive and hopeful. A number of people read my blog each time I publish an entry. I don't know who they are or why they choose to read it but that is the thing that interests me. It means that if people choose to they can find a lot more out about me, my thoughts, my dreams and my experiences.

I don't follow that many blogs myself but one I really enjoy is supposedly written by a pigeon called Brian. It is a hilarious portrayal of life according to a pigeon who starts off living in London but who travels further afield. Some famous people keep very popular blogs but I like the fact that you don't have to be famous to enjoy keeping a blog and to have people interested in reading what you have to say. Sometimes when I post my blog to Twitter I trigger the interest of people who share my interests.

Key words can trigger the interest of complete strangers. I wrote an entry about enjoying a glass of white wine only to find my tweet 'favourited' by someone who admires all things related to wine. I wrote about camping and found myself favourited by a camping enthusiast.

Try blogging for yourself. It is lots of fun!

48. Network Marketing:

A year or so ago I started thinking that there must be some other way of earning a living other than working full time, 40+ hours per week and so I started searching for alternatives. I came across all sorts of 'Get Rich Quick' schemes on The Internet. It is important to remember that if an opportunity seems too good to be true then it usually is. On the other hand there are some very viable alternatives to holding down a traditional 'job' that I have discovered.

Multi Level Marketing or MLM has been around for years. A few companies have been rather unscrupulous in their methods and have created Pyramid Schemes where people at the top earn money whereas people at the bottom make very little. These schemes have been banned and we are left with a good number of companies that offer a great service and provide opportunities for anyone who is willing to work hard and follow the tried and tested systems.

MLM has been active in the USA long before the UK so in the UK some people are a little suspicious and question the validity of the approach. Despite this, people who are open to new ideas are finding that there is a viable alternative to the 9-5. A good network marketing company offers value for money to its clients and treats its distributors fairly. If you think that you might like to get involved in MLM then go to a presentation to see what your role would involve.

I have become a distributor for 'Utility Warehouse Discount Club' which offer UK customers low cost utilities. Distributors are offered thorough training and a lot of support and encouragement. If a distributor signs up a customer they receive a bonus along with regular commission on their customers monthly bills. If they recruit distributors they also receive commission on their customer bills. The distributor receives on-going support from whoever recruited them. I am writing about this company because I have found them to be fair and effective. I am very glad I decided to work with them and the training I have received has benefited me in many other areas of my life.

This company and other MLM companies offer you the potential of earning residual income. Residual income is money that you receive long after you sign somebody up. In this example the commission received from customer bills continues as long as the customer remains with the company. Residual income increases as you gather more customers and can amount to a considerable sum of money. The beauty of MLM is that you can run it on a full or part time basis. It can be used to supplement your existing income, to provide you with luxuries or it can become your sole source of income.

I wanted to write about this because when I discovered MLM I realised that there are many different ways of doing things and that I am free to adopt different ways of working. This has a liberating affect on me as I have realised that I can earn money in different ways and ensure that I am doing what I enjoy doing. Maybe this would be a good way forward for you?

49. Your Heart:

Your heart is a very important organ, pumping blood around your body. You need your heart to work properly in order to survive. While it is possible to repair or replace your heart, it can certainly be described as a vital organ and requires a healthy diet and plenty of exercise to keep it in peak condition. You have probably heard the expression, "Don't let your heart rule your head."

People say that when they think that you are making decisions using your feelings rather than acting logically.

While I agree that it is important to take time and think about important decisions I do believe that we should consult our heart as well as our head. By this I mean that when I am thinking about applying for a new job I will definitely consider how I feel about the idea as well as thinking carefully about financial incentives, for example. Spending my time doing things that make me happy and help others to feel happy is very important to me. Of course I need money to live on but that is not my only consideration.

Some people choose to follow what have become known as 'heart centred' occupations. Roles have been created that help to bring joy to others as well as themselves. Becoming a nurse is an example of a fulfilling job role for someone that is definitely not solely motivated by earning money. There are easier ways to earn a living and there are jobs that earn a lot more money but people who decide to become a nurse often do so because they wish to make a positive difference to the lives of others.

An increasing number of grandparents give up well paid jobs to help their children bring up their families. They are motivated by love rather than money. I am not saying that you should adopt your heart as your only guide but I do feel that it should be considered when making important decisions.

50. Face Your Fears:

Fear is a unique experience. What frightens me may not frighten you. It is important to remember this when someone you know appears to be reacting over something that may seem trivial to you. Our fears can limit our lives. Agoraphobia, the fear of going out into open spaces can overtake a person's life to the point where they are afraid to leave their home, for example. This can severely limit what they are able to achieve in their lives.

Overcoming this fear and other fears can be very challenging but as with other challenges, starting with a tiny step is often the best way of overcoming them. Imagine someone has a fear of social situations such as parties. They may wish to start off by meeting a small group of people in a café for coffee before progressing to the more stressful party setting. For some people, friends and family might be able to help but sometimes professional help is needed in helping to identify stressful situations and suggesting possible remedies.

To find the right type of support for you it is a good idea to find out what is available in your area. Once you find a suitable therapist or counsellor build up the confidence to approach them for help. Managing to face your fears is liberating! Taking the first step can be frightening at first but as you take each small step it gradually gets easier until one day you suddenly realise that fear is no longer holding you back and you are finally living the life you choose.

51. Lack:

It is very difficult to see the bright side of life when you are short of money. It is all too easy to focus on what we haven't got rather than being grateful for the things that we do have. Adverts are designed to programme us to desire luxury products. They portray an idealised view of life filled with happy families living in beautiful homes. The adults drive the most up to date cars and can afford the most exotic holidays for themselves and their families. Models in magazines are airbrushed and perfect. Celebrities on TV sail in luxury yachts.

It is understandable that we sometimes compare our own lives unfavourably with the lives of others. We can feel depressed that we drive cheap cars, work long hours and are lucky if we are able to afford a bargain break.

If we do spend too much time focussing on what we haven't got we are likely to make ourselves miserable. If we are taken in by advertising, we are likely to be tempted to overspend and take out loans in an attempt to afford all the latest gadgets. Unless we are wealthy we can't compete with the luxury lifestyles of the super-rich.

It is important to remember that rich and famous people are not necessarily happy. You only have to read the celebrity magazines in order to realise that famous people have their fair share of unhappiness and that financial wealth can't buy you health.

Look at all the things that you have going for you. If you are in a happy family, you have a roof over your head, fresh water to drink and food in the cupboard, you are rich indeed. Focussing on lack brings you down while focussing on what is good about your life helps you to feel fulfilled.

52. Like Attracts Like:

What you give in life, you tend to receive. If you wish for something in your life, radiate it out to others and you are likely to receive it yourself. If you want to feel respected then treat people with respect. If you want to feel love then be loving to those around you and you will feel love in return. If you like to receive gifts, be generous to others and you will receive generosity and consideration from others.

Even during difficult times, if someone approaches you in an angry and argumentative mood and you treat them kindly and fairly they are more likely to calm and respond more positively to your kind treatment.

If you treat other people as you wish to be treated yourself, your life will begin to open up in exciting ways. It can be difficult to live this way when other people appear to be treating you unfairly but if you persevere your life will be enhanced.

Many people seem conditioned to gossip and speak negatively about others and when this happens around you it can be difficult to avoid getting sucked in. People that are consistently negative can bring you down and may be best avoided at times when you are feeling vulnerable.

Try going a day without complaining even once. It is a lot harder to achieve than you might initially think but if you persevere you will find that every aspect of your life starts to improve as you begin to focus on the most positive outcomes in every given situation. Once you achieve one positive day try why not try for another and then another until you achieve a positive week. Once a week has been achieved you can aim for a fortnight and then look back on your life and see how much happier you feel. You could even keep a note of your mood each day. You could score each day out of ten and see if your score improves throughout the process. I bet it does

53, Energy:

All living things comprise of energy. When we are filled with positive energy, we are more likely to attract good things into our lives. When our life experiences drag us down, our energy feels low and we can feel stuck. There are a number of therapies available that are designed to help us clear negative energy from our lives and help us feel healthier, happier and positive.

Christie Marie Sheldon provides Energy Clearing. It is said that different emotions vibrate on individual frequencies. Anger is said to have a low vibration while love has a high vibration, for example. The Beach Boys song 'Good Vibrations' adds weight to this theory.

The idea is that we can act to raise our vibrations to improve the quality of our lives.

Even if you do not accept that we experience positive and negative energy in this way, I think everyone agrees that we do experience ever-changing moods. Sometimes we are in a light and happy mood while at other times we feel rather fed up.

In order to feel more light hearted and happy there are some lovely visualisations that you can do. You can imagine healing light entering your body spreading throughout your body helping to put you in touch with the things that are truly important in life.

EFT Tapping can help us to release negative feelings in order to help us feel happy and attract more abundance into our lives.

On the other hand, watching too much bad news on TV or too many films of an aggressive or depressing nature can affect our mood. Eating fresh fruit and vegetables can restore our energy levels while drinking fresh water is beneficial. Breathing deeply out in the open air can restore our energy levels too.

I hope that this section has shown that there are a lot of things that we can do to help us feel positive and energised.

54. Re-frame Negatives:

Mother Theresa said that she would not attend an Anti-War rally. Instead she said that she would be happy to attend a Pro-Peace rally. To me this sums up a positive approach to life. Instead of fighting against Cancer how about starting a campaign for health? The way we frame things can make a lot of difference. Rather than focussing on the things we don't want in our lives why not think about the things that we do want?

Instead of thinking that you haven't got enough money try thinking about the money that you do have. Rather than pining away because we don't live in mansions we can appreciate the homes we do have. We may not be fast runners but many of us our lucky because we can walk.

It can be very beneficial to list three things that we are grateful for every day. Try explaining why you feel grateful for these things. Doing this daily and reviewing the things you have written on your list can help you to view the world in a more positive light. Avoid complaining and focus on gratitude and see how you life opens up. When things do go wrong there is no point in pretending that everything is wonderful if it is not. Instead accept that you are facing a challenging situation. Find ways of resolving the situation to achieve the most positive outcome, one step at a time.

55. Law Of Attraction:

I watched the film The Secret a few years ago. It spread the key message that 'Thoughts are Things.' What you focus on you attract. If you focus on attracting abundance into your life, positive people and situations will find their way to you. They will enable you to take inspired action to improve your life but if you focus on lack your life is likely to become more negative.

An increasing number of people have put the principals of The Law Of Attraction into practice. Many report that they have manifested positive outcomes. The idea is that you decide upon something you would like, such as a new job be specific about the kind of role that you would like.

The more vividly you picture things the more likely you are to be successful. When you put out your request to The Universe you do not have the tools you need initially. Once you 'place your order' the things and people needed to help you achieve your dream approach you. When the opportunities present themselves to you it is your task to take action. Take time each day to imagine what it will feel like when you achieve your dream, really feel it. The more often you do this the more motivated you will become and the quicker you will receive positive benefits. Failing to act on opportunities when they present themselves is likely to slow your progress.

The Law Of Attraction has proved powerful and can transform people's lives. Why not look into it yourself?

56. Inspirational Writers:

I am so grateful to the people who have dedicated their lives to improving the lives of others. Many have written books providing us with the opportunity of learning from them and transforming our own lives. Some authors have written books that have inspired millions throughout the world.

I find that as I read one book it points me in the direction of another book which in its turn points me towards another. Authors that have really stood out for me include Martha Beck with her book Steering By Starlight. She really explains how to follow our dreams in a way that resonates with me. Another wonderful author is Sonia

Choquette. Her book Soul Lessons helps each reader assess their own unique strengths and areas that they need to work on next. We all have areas of confidence and areas where we require more support.

Authors are dedicated and determined. Many of us have an idea for a book but lack the courage and determination to turn the dream into reality. It has taken me years to overcome my doubts and complete the process of writing a book from start to finish.

If you have a good idea for a book then please don't delay. You have a lot to offer the world and your words could offer vital support and encouragement to others. Start at the beginning, write a little each day and don't give up. That way your book will eventually find its way out into the world and it could change lives!

57. Inspirational Speakers:

Some people are inspirational speakers. I used to believe that certain people have a special gift and that speaking in public comes naturally to them and the rest of us should stick to talking to our friends and family on a much smaller scale. Since reading about the lives of some truly inspirational people, I have revised this view. I have discovered that many of these inspirational people are as scared of speaking in public as anyone else but that they have managed to overcome their fears in order to spread their important message to others.

I have been lucky enough to attend seminars where speakers have amazed me. I have also watched video's of people making inspirational speeches and the experience has enhanced my life. Lisa Nichols is one of the most memorable speakers that I have come across. She is so incredible because she is truly authentic. She is willing to share her story in order to help others. She talks of her struggle growing up and then bringing up her son in poverty. She resolved to change her life in order to provide for her son. She was able to use The Law of Attraction to manifest the things that she needed. Lisa asks her audience to visualise being a public speaker, sharing their message with the world. Each of us has our own unique story to tell. Lisa's message helps us to believe that if we can imagine it then we can do it.

A mistake many of us make is believing that we are insignificant. We are unimportant so why would other people be interested in hearing our story? Our lives are far from perfect and so we use this as an excuse to put off public speaking until we achieve perfection and since perfection is virtually impossible to achieve this gives us the perfect excuse to take no action.

Lisa's belief is that we all have our message for the world and that we can all inspire others so start small and build. When we stop thinking that we are unimportant we can start believing that we are unique and have our own gifts that we can begin to share with the world. If you have a message that you wish to share but don't know where to start then start small. Tell one or two people quietly. Whisper if you need to and gradually your whisper will turn into a shout and you will be able to get your message across to many!

58. Summits:

I work for a Network Marketing Business. Every 90 days they run some form of public event and we are all encouraged to attend. These events are intended to inspire, uplift and motivate. They work. Many organisations offer live events and summits in a similar way. This is because we all benefit from spending time and communicating with like minded, positive people.

Many of us may work alone and usually that is fine but every so often it is good to spend time with people who share your passion. That way you can benefit from their advice and support. It can provide you with the boost you need to keep on track and achieve more. It is good to know that you are not alone.

Hay House publish inspirational books. They also hold an annual summit. This features speakers and coaches from around the world.

Delegates can attend on-line live events. Attendees are introduced to new speakers and given the opportunity to hear from speakers on-line that they may never be able to see live. This cuts down on travel and accommodation costs and allows many thousands of people to benefit from the event.

Following The summit attendees are able to communicate with one another via a dedicated Facebook page. This is a great way for like minded people to continue to communicate, help and support one another on an on-going basis. Many tele-summits are free and can really help to enhance your life if you keep an open mind and give them a chance, I thoroughly recommend them.

59. Achieving Good Health~ Complimentary Medicine and Therapies:

Achieving good health is very important. If you have a healthy body and a healthy mind this forms an excellent basis for a happy life. Whatever your current state of health, it can always be improved. A healthy diet, a relatively stress-free life, drinking enough water, achieving a good work/life balance and regular exercise all help to promote good health. Despite all our best efforts there are times when we do become ill and our bodies require additional assistance in order to heal.

An accurate diagnosis is a useful starting point. Self-diagnosis achieved by looking up some symptoms on The Internet is not the safest or most effective course of action. It is often wise to seek out medical advice in order to quickly pinpoint what is wrong. Taking medical advice is often advisable. Most illnesses and conditions have a number of remedies so talk to your medical practitioner about alternative remedies if what they initially prescribe does not seem right for you. Many G.P.'s are happy for you to be treated by them alongside a complementary medical practitioner.

Many people benefit from the pain relief offered by Acupuncture, for example, while others greatly benefit from Aromatherapy, Reflexology and Homoeopathy. If you are taking a number of remedies, let your G.P. know so that one medication does not conflict with another.

I also find that remedies such as honey and lemon for colds and using tea-tree oil as an antiseptic work incredibly well for me. I am not recommending any particular course of treatment but I am pointing out that if you adopt an open-minded approach to achieving good health, there are a whole host of remedies that can really benefit you. Time spent researching in this area can be time very well spent.

60. Recycling:

Recycling is a great way of helping to preserve valuable resources. One person's rubbish is another person's treasure. I knew a group of people who decorated and furnished a house using reclaimed materials and they even found the paint to decorate the walls in a skip. When I was a child the recycling facilities that we have now were not in place but people still managed to repair items to prolong their life. They sold unwanted items cheaply at jumble sales and the proceeds were donated to worthwhile causes.

Now we also have boot-fairs and online auction sites including e-bay. If you have a large item of furniture you no longer require you can sell it cheaply online stating that the 'buyer collects' and that way you have an effective way of removing it at no cost to you.

It is easier to recycle now than ever before. Many places provide residents with a range of different bins so that unwanted items can be sorted and recycled. Clothes recycling bins are popping up everywhere. There are recycling facilities close to may supermarkets. When we give away or sell our unwanted items we are doing our bit to help preserve resources for future generations to come. This is a good message to teach our children too. If they see us mending and recycling things they are more likely to do the same in future.

61. Tiny Houses:

For a long time people believed that 'bigger must be better.' With rising living costs an increasing number of people are questioning this approach and are moving away from spending all their money on material possessions. They are electing to live a simpler life.

A movement that began in America is spreading across The Globe. It is 'The Tiny House Movement.' People have chosen to sell their large houses and move into tiny houses. Some people choose caravans or Park Homes, others live on boats and still others have adopted an eco-approach to building. There are a growing number of properties made out of recycled materials including using coloured glass bottles as a key component. One couple have managed to create a living/ working space in a tiny caravan with every millimetre of space is utilised so that they can incorporate everything that they need. Why do people make this decision?

Many have found that striving to fill their homes with all the must-have gadgets is not as fulfilling as they imagined and they start to crave the simpler things in life. They decide to spend time in the countryside or with their loved-ones. They choose to sacrifice space in order to conserve funds. That way they are able to spend their time and money pursuing the things that they enjoy the most. Other people choose to rent small and inexpensive homes in order to save money. This means that once they manage to save money they can take their first step on the housing ladder. They find that canal boats and caravans provide them with a great place to live while they save for a mortgage.

I have made the decision to live in a caravan and initially found it hard whittling down my possessions in order to fit into my own tiny house. Now I find that I love being there and don't miss any of the possessions I have parted with.

62. Green Politics:

I vote for The Green Party in local and national elections. Some people ask me why I choose to do this given that they are unlikely to receive enough votes to become the leading party. My view is that Green issues are important and if The Green Party do receive votes they will be able to influence decisions.

We cannot afford to neglect our planet. We must find ways in order to preserve resources for future generations. Developing Green energy alternatives such as wind, wave and solar power is crucial. Recycling and repairing things is also important. Working cooperatively and ensuring people from across the world are not exploited is very important to me. It is unfair that one group of people should profit at the expense of another.

Growing organic food is also important. Pesticide free food is better for our bodies and the Earth.

Recently a pesticide found to kill bees has been banned in some areas. Bees are a very important part of our biosphere. If bees do die out this would spell disaster for the future stability of our planet. I love the Native American Indian belief that we are put on Earth as caretakers of the land looking after the plants and animals for ourselves and for future generations. The Green Party is not in favour of intensive farming. To them animal welfare is the key.

To me a society is judged by the way that it treats vulnerable people and animals. Treating animals fairly and harmoniously and with respect is a positive way forward. Green policies promote equality and diversity. It is my hope that Green issues will play a big part in national and world politics to ensure our planet's healthy future.

63. Inclusion and Diversity:

I believe that everyone is equal. We are all unique individuals with our own gifts and talents. The role of Society should be to nurture and support each and every one of us so that we achieve our full potential. Some people are born with extra challenges such as physical and mental disabilities that can create barriers and obstacles for the individuals concerned. I feel that Societies role is to support individuals and provide them with the resources necessary in order to overcome these challenges.

It is unfair to treat someone negatively because of their gender, race or sexual orientation. Some people are afraid of the unknown. They can be quick to judge people that they know little about or they make snap judgements based on a person's physical appearance. If people are educated to value diversity and to learn about and respect one another's culture and beliefs, imagine how much more harmonious the world would become.

We can learn a lot from other people and can join together to support one another. Sharing our skills and talents with one another leads to a richer world. It is inspiring to watch people overcome their difficulties in order to achieve their goals. Watching the Paralympics is an example of how we can be inspired by watching people overcome significant disabilities to become the best that they can be.

64. Elderly Care:

Older people can feel excluded from our society. In the past, Elders felt more respected. Now some cultures appear to value their Elders more than others. Older people in the past had recognisable skills that they could pass on to future generations and as a result they were held in high esteem.

Now, in a time of rapid change and developing technology, it is the young and adaptable that are most valued. This is despite older people having incredible experience and wisdom. This can make older people feel excluded.

Many families struggle to care for their ageing relatives and are increasingly reliant on our Care system in order to look after their elderly relatives. An ageing population coupled with a period of slow economic growth is putting a strain on Care services. Some Care establishments appear to be able to pay and treat their staff fairly as well as offering residents a good standard of care while others are less effective.

While some families are able to visit their relatives frequently, many older people say that they that they feel lonely and isolated. They receive few visits. The reality is that older people have a lot of skills that they can teach us.

There are some excellent examples of good practice where Primary school pupils visit Care homes and the old and the young can benefit from being in each others company. There are also some Care homes that recognise the value of bringing animals in to spend time with their residents.

Older people have years of experience and a wealth of information to share with younger people. There are benefits for old and young alike when opportunities are created for them to spend regular time together. Many older people are still fit enough to volunteer for community projects and they have the time to devote. It is really important to recognise the talents of people of all ages in order to get the best out of people and to create a better world.

65. Permaculture:

Permaculture is a new way of growing food. A few years ago I went to visit a monkey sanctuary where I saw fruit trees growing in the woodland. Everything was organic and easy to manage. Each part helped to sustain another. Fruit bushes were sheltered from peak sun by the shade provided by the trees. Fallen leaves rotted down to make a nutritious leaf mulch. Rotten fruit from the fruit bushes were put into the compost and so on.

It is important that we turn our attention to sustainable living, particularly when it comes to the production of food. Intensive farming techniques mass produce crops that rely on increasingly strong pesticides. These have yet to be proven as safe in the long term. The survival of some insects, including bees, have been threatened by this increased use of pesticides.

If you turn a small part of your garden over to Permaculture you will be able to experience the pleasures and health benefits of growing your own fresh, organic produce. Beautiful flowers such as Nasturtiums can be grown alongside food crops to be used to repel pests and their wonderful flowers can be used to brighten and add interest to salads. It can be very beneficial to encourage young children to have their own vegetable patch but if you do not have a garden why not help them to grow plants in a window box?

If future generations can learn sustainable gardening techniques then the future of our planet will start to look rosier!

66. Religious Tolerance:

Tolerance is the key to unlocking a bright future for us all. There are many religions with diverse beliefs. Each will approach key areas in ways that appeal to a certain type of person. Many religions teach us to love one another and promote peace. These teachings can enhance our lives. A small minority preach hate and intolerance and serve to divide people.

Some of us are born into families who follow a particular religion and we decide to follow the same religion while some of us reject this and choose to follow another. Other people do not follow any particular religion and some may consider themselves to be spiritual but not religious. The important thing to remember is that we are all born, grow up and eventually die. We all experience degrees of happiness, sadness, riches and poverty.

One of the richest areas of life is when we reach out to and communicate with other people. We all have hopes and fears, joys and sorrows so we really aren't so different from each other. Listening to and learning about the lives of other people who experience a different culture or religion from our own is a good way to learn, grow and develop. If we try to set aside our differences and work together we can achieve great things.

It costs very little to research different religions and to find out more about other people's lives. Finding time to do this and making an effort to understand other people's viewpoints will bring us closer and serve to improve our lives. Many wars have been fought in the name of religion. Let us learn from the mistakes of the past so we can all live more harmoniously today.

67. Learning from Children:

We can learn so much from young children. They rarely spend their time worrying about things and they tend to live in the moment. They have a real lust for life. When it rains they squeal with delight and jump in all the puddles. When they are awake they are full of energy and enthusiasm. When they are tired they fall asleep. It is as simple as that.

Children are generally happy to play with anyone. They do not care about the colour of your skin or how rich you are. They say what they think and are usually disarmingly honest. I am a teacher. I have realised after years of working with children that despite what some of them say they do care what you think. A careless word said to a child when they are young can affect them adversely in future years. Many people remember being told that they couldn't sing when they were young and this can put them off singing for life. Other people were told they couldn't draw and so they gave up trying.

When children are young they are usually eager to try new things, to paint, to draw, to dance and sing. It is not until an adult passes judgement on their work that it even occurs to them that they might not be good at something. Young children often start off thinking that they can achieve great things. I believe that it is our responsibility to encourage their creativity and their self-belief. We can all be singers, dancers and artists if we choose to be!

68. Learning from Older People:

You can learn so much from older people. As I grew up I was fascinated by both sets of grandparents. Between them, they had so much life experience. Combined experiences include travelling the world, serving in the army, being a postman, growing vegetables and riding to work on a bike. One granddad was a Cinematographer and prior to that his job had been to feed the milkman's horse its hay. One grandmother abandoned her family and religion leaving India to marry my granddad. She moved to the UK. My other grandparents retired and lived in a country cottage in a little village near Wales. There were horses living in the fields behind them and stickleback swam in the river. Listening to their stories and spending time with these people helped to create my childhood and I wouldn't swap these experiences for the world.

Many interesting people from every walk of life are now living in Care homes living out their final years. If you take the time to fully listen to older people you will benefit from learning about their rich experiences and this will enhance your life. We all have our own unique histories and no life is dull. Older people also have the benefit of wisdom gained from many years of life experience. We have a lot to learn from the people who came before us. Listening to them stops us repeating the mistakes of the past and can lead to a more positive future.

69. Give Up Unhappiness:

Yes I am asking you to give up your unhappiness, to fully let it go. Now this may sound silly or difficult at first but I am asking you to stop, take a breath and pinpoint how you feel right now. If you conclude that you are feeling unhappy then I think it is safe to say that the source of your unhappiness is likely to be something that has occurred in the past. If not then it is probably something that you are worried might happen in the future. Now is where you are. The longer you are able to spend living in the present moment, the happier you are likely to be.

If you feel that your unhappiness does come from the past and there is no action that you can take to ease this unhappiness then let it go. Whatever your problem, let it go. If your partner has left you for example, allow yourself to grieve for your loss, release your sadness, let it go.

Try EFT Tapping to release negative energy and focus on your present life. Truly look around you. Look at the things, situations and people you have in your life now. Focus on them and gradually you will feel happier. If you are unhappy because you fear something may occur in the future and there is an action that you can take to prevent this from happening then take action now. If there is nothing that you can actively do to resolve things then focus on Now. Be in this moment and you will find the inner reserves that you need to handle any situation.

The fear of something is often worse than the actual thing. The more you are able to let go and to live in the present moment the better you will feel. Living in the present provides you with the tools necessary to act quickly when you need to and to respond positively to the events that are happening in your life. Meditation can really help you do develop the skill of living Now. Why not give it a try?

70. Clothes:

Clothes can reflect aspects of your personality. Rather than going to expensive boutiques you can go to jumble sales, boot-fairs and charity shops to buy items that you like and then you can adapt or accessorise them to suit your taste. You don't need to be a dress-maker to make small changes to clothing to make it suit you more or fit you better. If you have clothes that you no longer wear then consider donating them or swapping them for clothes that you do like.

Increasingly people enjoy attending swapping parties where they bring unwanted clothes and exchange them for garments that friends have brought in that suit them better. Another persons cast-offs could well turn out to be one of your favourite new clothes. Different colours suit certain people. Don't worry about conforming to this season's colours, particularly if they don't suit you. Don't wear this season's fashions unless you enjoy wearing them. Instead, wear what you like and enjoy becoming known for your own unique style.

Another lovely thing to do with unwanted garments is to turn them into part of a patchwork. Many people have clothes that they no longer wear but they still like the pattern of the material or the item holds good memories. Using the fabric to make another item is an excellent way of continuing to enjoy the fabric instead of cramming it into a wardrobe where it remains for years taking up space and is never worn.

71. Boot-fairs, Jumble Sales and Second Hand Shops.

I love boot-fairs. They are filled with motivated early-risers who have all sorts of interesting things to sell. I have had many stalls at boot-fairs. I have learnt a lot about buying and selling there. On the days when I am feeling relaxed and cheerful I usually have a steady flow of customers and on days when I feel out of sorts or desperate to sell certain items I find that customers tend to stay away.

I enjoy attending boot-fairs in all seasons. Being wrapped up warm looking for novelty items as Christmas approaches is fun as is getting up early on a summer's morning to browse for something unique.

Boot-fairs provide us with a great opportunity to make money and to save money. I once found a excellent pair of shoes at the end of a boot-fair when the stalls were packing up. One stall holder didn't want to take many items home with them so they left unwanted items on a blanket with a sign that said 'free please take.' Those shoes fitted me perfectly and lasted me a long time. I enjoy loading my car with books and other items that I no longer require and selling them at boot-fairs. When people buy the books that I have enjoyed reading I like the fact that other people will experience that same enjoyment. Some people sell delicious food and others sell plants.

Boot-fairs are like an Aladdin's cave of interesting items just waiting to be explored. Give them a try some time. Jumble sales are a good way for charity organisations to make money. They can ask for donations of clothes that are sold cheaply. Charity shops also welcome donations of good quality second hand clothes. The charity benefits when the item is sold and people living on a low income can gain from buying clothes inexpensively in this way.

72. Volunteering:

Volunteering has many benefits. Many people like to volunteer and the service that they provide is invaluable to others. Some people volunteer in charity shops and some become hospital visitors.

Volunteering can enhance the quality of your life as well as the lives of the people that you are able to help. Some people volunteer while unemployed and the experience they gain can help them find employment. A lot of people volunteer after retiring. They find themselves with time on their hands and they decide that they would like to make a difference by helping other people. Some people volunteer to forget their own difficulties by focussing on other people and their needs. Volunteer positions can be exciting, demanding, challenging and rewarding. Don't knock it until you try it. I enjoy the experience of volunteering. Doing something because I choose to and not because I have to do it in order to get paid.

If you are interested in Volunteering, look in the local paper or carry out an Internet search to see what is available in your area. Some volunteer opportunities are advertised in shop windows.

Local hospitals regularly have volunteer positions. If you aim to work with children or vulnerable adults then you will need to be vetted. Some voluntary positions offer expenses for food and travel. You will be told about the terms and conditions when you apply. If you do decide to go ahead take your role seriously, be punctual and reliable as people will be depending on you. You will find that volunteering is one of the most satisfying, rewarding ways of spending your free time.

73. Dreaming:

Many cultures find dreams to be highly significant. Some symbols from dreams can represent things in real life. There are websites devoted to dream interpretation. I go through periods of not really remembering my dreams and then I experience periods of vivid dreaming where I recall every detail. I try to write down my dreams as soon as I wake up as it is surprising how quickly I forget them again.

If you want to try and work out what your dream means to you you can try focussing on an aspect of your dream. Imagine I dream that a dog starts chasing me when I am walking to the shop. I could try asking the dog why it was chasing me and the dog might answer. I could question other elements of the dream such as the shop. I know that this sounds odd but humour me. I have tried this myself. I have asked elements of my dream what they are trying to show me and then sometimes an answer pops into my head. The answer can sometimes reveal the answer to a dilemma.

An example of this was when I was dreaming about a tree that was blowing in the wind on the edge of a cliff. I asked the tree what it was doing in my dream and it replied that it was being flexible, bending in the wind so it wouldn't snap. I interpreted this as me needing to 'go with the flow' at work as sometimes this is the best option.

Next time you find yourself puzzling over the meaning of a dream try asking the elements of your dream for answers and you may be surprised at what is revealed.

74. Sculpture:

I enjoy sculpture. Years ago I took an art A level and as part of my studies I experimented with clay. I created a 3 Dimensional form, glazed it, fired it and admired the end results. I went to Art College and enjoyed experimenting with unusual materials involving plaiting hay to make hangings. There is something very satisfying about working in 3D. I started to miss making sculpture when I got a job as a nursing assistant. I loved my job but I didn't feel that I was nurturing my creative side and so I enrolled on a sculpture course. It was run as an evening class and I really enjoyed it. This time I experimented with carving plaster blocks. I created some 'Modern Art.' It was a plaster model of a man with his arm outstretched holding onto an umbrella that had blown inside-out in the wind. The spokes were all bent out of shape.

If you have never tried sculpture, I really recommend that you try it. My dad turned out to be very good at wood carving when he decided to try it. He would never have known if he hadn't enrolled on a taster course. He enjoyed it and discovered that he had a talent. He has made me a beautiful wood carving of Pegasus the winged horse. It hangs proudly in my home.

Making a sculpture certainly doesn't have to be expensive. You can make very effective sculptures using recycled, unwanted and found objects. The beach is an excellent place to find interesting shaped driftwood that can be turned into something unique.

75. Animal Sanctuaries:

There are a number of animal sanctuaries across the world. They have different animals and individual arrangements but what they have in common is a wish to look after unwanted animals and to give them a second chance in life. A high number of animals are found neglected and abandoned by their owners. The sanctuaries often rely on donations in order to survive. They also ask volunteers to come in and help with the animals including cleaning out, feeding and exercising the animals.

Other people fund-raise to help the sanctuaries raise much needed money. They hold jumble sales and raffles in order to raise money. Some people buy a new puppy without thinking of the long term implications. As the puppy grows and becomes an adult dog they can find that having the dog does not fit in with their lifestyles.

Sometimes family events such as the birth of a new baby can lead people to decide that they can no longer keep the dog. The dog gets handed in to a sanctuary and the search begins for a new owner. If you are thinking of getting a dog or a cat maybe you could consider giving an unwanted animal a new home instead of buying a puppy or kitten from a shop. Animals from sanctuaries come to you neutered and vaccinated. They are often house trained and used to living with people. They can make excellent pets. Don't they deserve another chance?

76. Bread Making:

Have you ever made your own bread? It can be very satisfying. It is a lovely thing to teach a young child to do. They really enjoy kneading the dough and leave it to rise. You can make bread from scratch or you can use a bread maker. There are a large range of flour to choose from when baking your bread and you can make speciality bread such as Ciabatta. It can be fun to add seeds and other ingredients to the bread. I like adding pumpkin seeds or olives.

The smell of baking bread is very appetising when you come into someone's home. Supermarkets have caught on to this and often bake their own bread in order to attract customers and encourage them to spend more in their store.

Home baking can be very satisfying and makes a pleasant change from relying on preprepared products from Supermarkets. Young children can have great fun making then eating their own bread. If you take the time to teach them how to do this they will enjoy the precious time spent with you and they will have learnt an important skill that they can pass on to others in future.

77. Wine Making:

I enjoy making my own wine. It is definitely something interesting and satisfying to do. I bought a heated pad and some demijohns when I began making wine. I enjoyed picking fruit such as plums and blackberries in order to make the wine. I added sugar and yeast and the process began. It is lovely watching the bubbles glugging away in the demijohn as the wine ferments. It takes time but it is well worth the wait.

It is good fun serving the wine to friends when it is ready. The red wine can be very rich and strong. Some batches almost taste like sherry. White wine tends to be lighter and easier to drink. I love gooseberry and elderflower. Being able to choose unusual ingredients is part of the fun.

It makes a change from the more conventionally made wine available in supermarkets. You can make pretty labels and give the wine away as a gift. You can branch out and make your own beer too. This hobby can be shared with friends. You can each make your own wine or beer and then share it with one another when it is ready. For people who do not enjoy alcohol it is fun to make elderflower cordial and other non alcoholic beverages using natural ingredients.

78. The Gift of Time:

One thing that is precious and sometimes seems in short supply is Time. Everyone benefits from being listened to and cared for. In our fast-paced modern times, many parents work long hours and return home exhausted with little time left to spend with their children.

Parents often work overtime to earn extra money to buy their children expensive gifts. They don't always realise that the very best gift that they can give their child is their time.

Many of us would have liked to attend a club or activity when we were young and perhaps our parents refused this saying they didn't have enough money. Maybe that is why many parents are determined that their child will want for nothing and so they spend many hours working in order to be able to afford exciting holiday and after-school activities for their children. These activities are fun and their child may well enjoy them but for many children, what they really want is to spend time with their parents, talking with them and having fun.

The same applies to older people. A little quality time spent with older people reaps dividends.

Your time is a precious commodity. Use it wisely. You may not realise how important you are to the people around you.

79. Bees and Other Insects:

Every plant and animal plays a unique part in our biosphere. The honey bee plays a much more significant role than you might think. They are pollinators and therefore without them some plants may not reproduce. Bees are sensitive to pesticides that we use and as a result many have died out. There are so many insects in the world and we know relatively little about them. We call them pests when they live too close to us.

Clothes moths would be an example of an insect that we find hard to tolerate. Their caterpillars eat fabric causing a lot of damage to the family home. Despite this these insects have interesting life cycles. Inspects are an important part of the food chain. Without them many species of bird would be threatened. Animals that reply on the birds as prey would be threatened and so on.

I like the fact that insects live alongside us and are easily accessible. Children love finding out about them. In schools bug-hunts are held so that children can learn all about their habitats and life cycles. It is important for children to learn about the world around them and to treat other creatures with respect. If we show interest in insects and react calmly when we encounter them then our children are more likely to like and respect them too.

We are so busy these days that we can find it hard to take time out to watch a butterfly gathering nectar from a flower. Look around you now. There is bound to be an insect close by. Take a little time out to look at it and appreciate it. Often if we can focus on tiny things it helps us make sense of the big things. This can help us to put our problems into perspective. We are rather like tiny insects in the grand scheme of things. Despite our fears life goes on around us so why worry so much?

80. Birds:

There are many different types of birds and I am particularly interested in the ones I see everyday. Some birds migrate in winter and others remain local. People like to put out food for them in winter and watch them from their windows. This can be very helpful for the birds during a hard winter and it can also be extremely beneficial for us.

Watching Nature can help to calm us, to ground us even.

Some birds have adapted to the urban environment altering their feeding habits in order to live off scraps left around by humans. Seagulls and pigeons have proved themselves to be particularly adaptable in this way. Pigeons have become so successful living in towns that they have become regarded as pests. They are intelligent and adaptable and their population is increasing. Seagulls have moved inland and have discovered that there are many tasty morsels to be gleaned from people's rubbish. Large populations are appearing near landfill sites so that they are able to feast from our left-overs.

Even in the most built-up environments birds live alongside us. I enjoy looking out for the similarities and differences between birds I see where I live and the birds that I have spotted in other countries. We can gain a lot of pleasure from watching birds in their natural environment. There are hides in nature reserves that are free to visit. Even if we can't leave the house it is usually possible to hang a bird feeder up outside the window so we can watch the birds come and go. Encouraging children to spot birds and look them up in a bird book can really help to teach them to appreciate the world around them and is a very inexpensive thing to do. My parents taught me the names of some common birds and even now I really enjoy spotting them when I am out and about.

81. Seasons:

There are four seasons and each season brings its own uniqueness. In some parts of the world the change in season is more dramatic than others. Spring is a beautiful season in UK. It marks the beginning of new life. As the weather warms up and the days get longer the bulbs start to shoot up and the animals give birth to their young.

Summer sees a rise in temperature and even longer days. People tend to take time off work and spend time on holiday with their families. Autumn sees the leaves on the trees changing colour. The nights start to get longer and the temperature colder. The winter can often bring snow and long dark nights. We find ways of celebrating each season.

Religions have different celebrations in winter. Christians have Christmas and in Spring they celebrate Easter. Diwali marks the start of the Hindu New Year. There are a number of religions and each has their own celebrations. People who do not belong to any religion still celebrate the changing seasons. Halloween is enjoyed by millions of people, as is Bonfire Night. We find our own personal reasons to celebrate too.

Some people hold an annual barbecue to celebrate a family occasion such as a birthday. We adapt our celebrations according to the time of year. In UK the weather can be unpredictable. People hold outdoor weddings in summer but make sure they have a marquee in case it rains.

I love the fact that despite all our advanced technologies, we are still affected by the weather. I have a caravan sited on a cliff. I love looking down at the waves crashing below and staring at the black storm clouds gathering. Lying awake at night, listening to the rain hammering down on my caravan roof makes me happy. I feel cosy indoors and full of awe at the power of the storm. Thunder storms can be incredibly dramatic and so can the colours of a mid summer sunset. We cannot change the weather so why not enjoy and appreciate it anyway? Teaching our children to enjoy all seasons can enhance their lives.

Many of us have happy memories of building a snowman in winter or paddling in the sea in summer. Appreciating the changing seasons and every kind of weather enhances our happiness all year round.

'Surround yourself with Nature.'

82. Seasonal Food:

In the past we tended to eat different things in the changing seasons. These days, if we go to a supermarket we can buy any food that we like all year round. Is this necessarily a good thing? It makes sense to eat food as it becomes available. Salads in Summer, root vegetables in the Autumn and warming stews in Winter. Eating seasonal fruit is also delicious.

We can enjoy strawberries and ice-cream in Summer, plum or rhubarb crumbles in Autumn. Each season brings its own wonderful produce and eating it fresh is the best. If I buy a strawberry out of season it never tastes as good. Why not buy what is freely available now? It is usually cheaper and cuts down on polluting our planet by transporting food around the world.

Consider buying from a farmers market knowing that you are supporting local farmers. Most of the food that you buy there is organically produced and completely fresh.

There are a number of delicious recipes that use ingredients according to the gluts of the season. When marrows are ready to pick you can end up with a bumper crop. Why not try out different recipes and choose your favourite? You can make large batches of food and freeze what you don't need so that you can enjoy the food long after the season has passed. This is a good way of cutting down on waste and saving money. It can also be great fun cooking new recipes and asking friends and family to sample what you have made. You can swap popular recipes with other people which is a great way of receiving exciting new recipes yourself.

83. Craft:

A lot of my friends are really good at making things. They enjoy making handmade cards or knitting unique items. Some people spin and dye their own wool while others are very good at making their own clothes. Traditional arts and crafts are fun to make and wonderful to buy. Some people start off with a hobby which builds into a business.

It is lovely to buy hand crafted gifts for friends and family. They receive something unique and you have the fun of visiting the craft events and selecting something beautiful at the same time as supporting local crafts people. It is so nice to receive a thoughtful hand-crafted gift.

There are regular craft markets that are wonderful to visit. I enjoy going to Greenwich Market where stall holders sell cards and other hand crafted items as well as delicious food. There is bound to be something similar in your local area. It is great to support local craftspeople.

If you admire something, talk to the stall holder about their work. If they are not too busy they will be happy to talk about their passion.

They may inspire you to take up a craft yourself. There are companies that sell craft materials inexpensively. Why not give it a try yourself. You may discover a talent that you didn't know you had. In time it could even be you running a popular stall selling your own beautiful creations. Trying something out costs very little and can lead to a richer, fuller life.

84. Celebration Cakes: Making People Feel Unique:

When my children were little, I used to make their birthday cakes. Each year I would think of something that they might like and I would try and create a cake to represent it. As they grew older, I would ask them what they would like for their birthday cake. The wonderful thing was that they had total belief that I could make anything. They had no doubt in my ability to make whatever they asked for. Each year I tried my best to create what they requested. One year I made a Barbie cake. Another year I made a hedgehog cake. We went to Venice to celebrate my daughter's eighteenth birthday and so I made a Gondola cake that year. I am not much of a cook but I really enjoy making celebration cakes.

I make my own Christmas cake and Christmas pudding every year. I don't even weigh out the ingredients any more and each year I vary the type of dried fruit I put into them. Some cakes come out more tasty than others but I enjoy eating each one all the same. I think making the cake is one of my favourite aspects of Christmas. To me it is symbolic of Christmases past when everyone made things for themselves. It represents the way people used to live, gathering then drying and storing fruit in Summer and Autumn so that it could be preserved for the winter.

You can get a lot of satisfaction from making your own cakes, it costs very little so why not give it a try?

85. Values:

We all have our own values and one of the most important things in our lives is working out what they are. Once we have worked out our values we can try and live our lives according to them. Core values are the ones that we hold dear. They are non negotiable. It can be beneficial to write down our core values in the form of our own personal Mission Statement. It takes time to work out what we really do stand for but once we know that we are clearer on who we are and what we wish to promote. We can really progress. A life lived according to our core values is likely to be a rich and happy life.

If we are expected to do things that conflict with our core values we are likely to make ourselves miserable. This can happen at work. If we are asked to do something that we feel uncomfortable about we are faced with a choice. We can try and persuade our boss to let us off or refuse to comply and risk potentially losing our job. The other option might be to reluctantly do as we are told. Only we can decide what the right course of action is for us.

In order to work out your core values you can write down the things that make you happy, the things that make you sad. You can record the things that you think are right with the world and the things that you believe are wrong. Write down everything that you think of and then look back at your list. Look at what you have written and see what really stands out for you. Some things are likely to be more important to you than others. You will probably see four or five things that really stand out for you on your list. They are likely to be your core values.

If you live your life according to your core values you are likely to feel happier and more fulfilled. Sometimes we don't realise that our values have been violated until after the event. The way we know that our values have been compromised is by working out how we feel about something. It is hard to ignore our feelings. We take action and our actions have consequences. Once we have acted we are able to look back and see how we feel about our actions. If we feel unhappy we can review and assess what we can do differently. If necessary we can take action to put things right.

Living life according to our values need not cost money and leads to a fuller life. Trying to live in a way that conflicts with our core values is likely to lead to misery If you struggle to work out what changes you can make to live life according to your core values then you could consider contacting a coach. They will be able to help you identify the things that matter to you. They can assist you in deciding what changes you wish to make and will help you identify measurable goals to help you achieve a happier life.

86. Community Living:

In our modern times we move at a fast pace. We work long hours and strive to buy material things. As a result of this, some of us seem to have lost our sense of community. A lot of us don't really know our neighbours and tend to keep ourselves to ourselves.

Some people, by contrast, know their neighbours well. They look out for them and are around to celebrate their joys or commiserate with their sorrows. We can learn a lot from these people. It is important that everyone has a support network around them. People that they can turn to when they need help. This does not cost us anything and the rewards can be remarkable.

In our society, many families have moved apart from one another. When people need help they are often forced to call upon Social Services to help them. The number of people requiring support, particularly when they get older, has put strain on our services. This is leading to spiralling Health and Care costs.

I hope that there will come a time where our society slows down and realises how vital it is to look after people in need. People who choose to care for their friends and family should be supported financially themselves. To me, a society is judged on how it looks after its citizens.

We can all do small things to help others. Helping can be as simple as holding a door open for someone who is struggling to get through it. The important thing is to be observant and sensitive to the needs of the people around us. Even smiling at someone who is looking a little down can be a great help. Often we don't ever get to hear how we have helped another person.

I remember a teacher who listened to me and allowed me to go to her classroom and draw pictures when I was feeling down. I was feeling sad because my mum had recently died. I didn't want to talk about it but I did need help. I needed someone to notice me and give me some time and space to be myself. That teacher realised this. It cost her nothing and made all the difference to me. I never told her what a difference she made to my life back then but I won't forget her.

If you take time to notice how others are feeling and listen to them when they need to talk it will cost you nothing and could help them more than you will ever know.

87. Thoughtful Gifts:

One Spring day at work, I was given some Easter eggs unexpectedly. Another time I found a postcard given to me by some old work colleagues. It was given to me when I left my job and the messages were very thoughtful. These two gifts really put a smile on my face.

Gifts do not have to be expensive. It really is 'the thought that counts.' When my children were little I used to love receiving home made Mothers Day gifts. I have kept some of the gifts, the cards and drawings they made for me. I am pretty sure Gran who is in her 90's still has some of the drawings I made for her when I was little.

Advertising would have us believe that expensive designer gifts is all we crave but if you talk to most people it is the hand made personal gifts that matter most.. While it is nice to receive a gift on Valentine's day it can be even nicer to receive a spontaneous gift on another day.

You don't have to wait until someone's birthday to buy them a gift or better still you can make the a gift. Even a simple hand written note thanking someone for the things they do for you can be very much appreciated. The gifts that make me the happiest are the gifts given by people who have really thought about what I might like. If you are short of money you can make or buy a gift from someone that costs little but means a lot if you take time to work out the likes and interests of the person you wish to surprise.

88. Change Begins With You:

Many of us would like to change some aspect of our lives. We may wish to move house or meet someone new. We might want a better job or more money and we may begin to feel resentful when we don't receive the things that we want. We may be annoyed that our partner does not help us enough or that our children never seem to want to talk to us. We could really want change and feel frustrated when we don't get it. If you want change the best place to start is with yourself.

What I have learnt is that if I behave the way I always have I will continue to get what I always have but if I approach things differently I am more likely to achieve a different outcome. If we take a step back and try and see our situation from another person's point of view we can sometimes see ourselves as other people regard us. This can be very helpful.

If we are feeling brave we can ask another person for feedback. We can ask someone that we respect if they can suggest ways that we can approach things differently. It is hard for us to change the way that we do things but if we can reflect on our own behaviour we can sometimes see ourselves from another person's point of view and then we can adapt our approach.

Becoming a better listener is a great way of bringing about change. When another person speaks to us it is tempting not to listen fully and to be mentally preparing our response to them. If we can stop doing this and really listen to the other person they will notice the difference. If you listen carefully to what people are really saying and allow yourself time to respond genuinely, your communication with them will improve dramatically. You are likely to improve your relationship with them. This should lead to more positive outcomes for all concerned.

If you want change, change yourself.

89. Colours:

We all have our favourite colours. We choose different colours for the walls in our houses and the furnishings. We have colours that we enjoy wearing and colours that people say suit us best. Some people choose different coloured lighting to enhance mood. Our mood definitely seems to be influenced by colour and due to this, thought is given to the colour walls are painted in public areas. Hospitals choose light colours including cool blues and soft greens. It is rare that public toilets are painted bright red as red represents danger and creates the wrong ambience.

I love looking at the different colours in sunsets and during the changing seasons. In Spring, leaves are fresh green and as Summer comes they become darker. When Autumn arrives the leaves on trees can turn deep red, fiery gold or vibrant orange.

Even if you are not much or an artist it can be fun buying paint and experimenting with colour mixing. Colour therapists are available to help us choose colours that suit our skin tone and enhance our mood. Fashions come and go and there are different colours to reflect the changing seasons. It can be fun to wear the on-trend colours but we don't need to be ruled by them. If we find an item of clothing that we like to wear it does not matter if the colour is not 'this season's colour.' Be yourself. Surround yourself with the colours that make you happy.

90. Second Hand Clothes:

In the past it was the norm to buy clothes for one child then pass them on to another child. In modern times people seem to have moved away from this and buy new clothes for each child.

I think this is a shame. While it is nice to have new things, why not pass on second hand clothes if they are in good condition so that they can be appreciated in the future?

I am not the only person to believe this. There are lots of people who like to buy second hand clothes from boot-fairs and charity shops. There are also people who buy second hand clothes and resell them after revamping them by adding accessories such as beads etc. Why not buy second hand clothes if they are in good condition and well made?

Recently there has been a rise in the number of shops selling vintage clothes as people have become interested in the 1940's and 1950's fashions. These clothes can be expensive so if you are good at dress making you could buy fabric from a second hand shop then make your own for a fraction of the price. If, like me, you are not very good at sewing why not swap skills with someone who is? If you are good at baking you could bake for someone who is good at sewing. In return they can make the garment that you want. Thinking creatively in this way can save money and bring people closer together.

91. Mending:

If something is broken we throw it away. This appears to be what most people do these days and this approach is contributing to landfills full of junk. Earth's resources are depleting at a rapid rate. In the past, particularly during times of war when resources were scare, a 'make do and mend' approach was adopted. Peopled darned socks with holes in and took down a hem to make a skirt last longer.

Manufacturers today appear to be making it harder to fix things. Many shops sell items that do not last long, they are designed to be thrown away. Despite this we all have items that could be repaired if we took the time to fix them.

If we don't have the skills to fix things we may know someone who can. Some people have started their own businesses offering to repair clothes, for example. All I am saying is that next time something breaks, why not see if it can be repaired? Some people enjoy repairing things as a hobby. Many people like building computers using parts from old and broken machines. Other people like to repair old cars.

If we all take time to consider if we can repair our broken items or give them to some one who likes fixing things then we will be able to change the 'throw away culture' and create something more sustainable.

92. Swapping:

If you have an item of clothing that you used to like but now it no longer fits you, why not swap it instead of throwing it out? People are starting to see the benefit of swapping their unwanted items.

In times of economic difficulty we struggle to afford new things for ourselves but if we bring along our unwanted clothes to a 'swapping party' we can exchange them for clothes that we do like.

This approach does not have to be limited to clothes. We can swap books, CD's, anything! When swapping items make sure that they are clean and well presented. Clothes should be put on a hanger and their size clearly labelled. Any special instructions such as washing guidelines should also be displayed.

If there are no swapping events where you live, why not consider running one yourself? You could start by inviting a few friends round but then if you enjoy it you could expand and run swapping parties for your local community, perhaps in a community centre. Items should be displayed clearly. It makes sense to group items according to size.

That way people can visit a clothes-rail containing items in their size so that they have a good range of items to choose from. Electrical items need to be safety tested and CD's need to be scratch free.

People attending the swapping parties need to be informed which items are suitable to bring and how they should be presented. That way everyone attending the event will know what to expect and are more likely to benefit from the experience.

93. Libraries:

Libraries are still alive and well in many parts of the country. When I was a child everyone used their local library. We had a ticket that entitled us to take out around three books from an enormous range. We could borrow the books for about a month and if we wanted to borrow them for a little longer we could phone the library and arrange to have the books renewed.

Now things have moved on somewhat. You can borrow e-books and you no longer need to get the books stamped but the principle is the same. My local library has had a makeover. It has a café and a range of community leaflets that you can look through.

Books can be ordered in for you to read. Many libraries offer access to archived information and some allow you to book time on their computers. Why not call in to your local library and see what is available where you live. If you are new to a place the local library is a good place to go to start to get to know your new local area. Many community groups advertise their services there and you may be able to find some events of interest to you advertised there. Books are wonderful they provide us with information and inspire us with the thoughts and ideas of people who were here before us.

Even at times of dire need, a library can be a sanctuary. It provides a comfortable, dry place to go during the day and offers us the chance to learn new things. Visiting the Children's Section of the library can be great fun for small children. You can have a lovely time browsing the books and you can find out which books they really enjoy. Once you know their favourite book characters you know what you can get them for a lovely gift.

94. Grown Your Own:

It is so easy to call into a Supermarket and buy whatever you want but despite this there is nothing quite like 'growing your own.'

You can buy seeds even if you only have a window box and you can grow your own herbs, peppers or tomatoes. If you have a small garden you can grow lettuces, carrots and radishes.

Consider growing your own flowers too. It is lovely to have a vase of cut flowers brightening up your home knowing that they were grown in your garden. If you grow your own flowers you can choose from a large range of seeds and a great variety of flowers. If you buy a bunch of flowers from a shop you are limited to the most popular varieties. I love Sweet Peas. You can't really buy bunches of them in a flower shop but you can grow and pick your own.

You can grow unusual or old fashioned varieties of fruit and vegetables. Many of these are not available in Supermarkets. Encouraging children to grow their own fruit and vegetables is great fun and they take real pleasure in eating the food that they have grown. Schools are waking up to the benefits of encouraging children to grow their own food. It is a great way of encouraging children to 'eat their greens.'

95. Writing Letters:

We don't tend to write many letters any more. We usually send emails and 'phone or text our friends. While this is quick and convenient I do feel that we have lost something by doing this.

During The War, Sweethearts would write to each other and soldiers would wait eagerly to receive hand-written letter's from their loved ones. If you go to museums you will see examples of letters and postcards that were written during those difficult times.

I still write to my grandmother. She is in her nineties. She tells me that she doesn't mind me sending emails if I am busy but I still write her a real letter every few weeks. I love getting her letters in return. Why not surprise someone and write them a letter. It could make their day? There are a range of inexpensive and attractive note-lets available from shops.

Receiving real cards can be so much nicer than receiving an e-card. Making the card can be better still. There are companies that invite you to personalise their cards with your own photo or message. These cards are popular as they are professional looking yet unique. Receiving letters and cards makes us feel closer to our friends and family who may live far away. Some people enjoy collecting the stamps that they receive. Stamps from different countries are very attractive and striking. These can be collected and appreciated in their own right.

96. Buy Locally:

There are a lot of small businesses in your local area that are struggling to survive. This is not because they offer poor quality products but because they are competing with huge Multi-Nationals and without your support they may go out of business. This applies to food shops, craft shops, toy shops, book shop, music shops, you name it. There are local craft and farmer's markets selling good quality produce. Why not go and look round them and see what they offer?

I am not saying that we should spend lots of money on inferior products just because they are local. What I am saying is take the time to see what is available on your doorstep and make an informed choice. I am not anti Supermarket. They provide us with a huge range of affordable items but I do feel that if we do not support local businesses now they may disappear and then we will lose out as there will be less choice and less variety in life.

97. Recycling services:

When I moved house recently I needed to get rid of lots of possessions as I was down-sizing. I sold what I could, gave away what I could and then contacted a local charity who specialises in collecting furniture and selling it cheaply to people in need. They collected a number of items of furniture for free and then sold it to people who needed it.

There are also organisations such as Free-cycle who put people in touch with each other. It advertises items that people want to give away and then if you need something you can contact them and collect the items you need. This means that people can give away what they no longer need without throwing things away. Next time you want to get rid of something why not consider Free-cycling it?

https://www.freecycle.org/

98. What Makes a Society?

This is a big question. What makes a society?

To me the way a society treats its citizens is what makes or breaks a society. I believe that people should be entitled to a free education, a good health care system and somewhere safe and secure to live. A caring society looks after people in need and helps people to live as independently as possible.

Look around you. Look at what is good and bad about the community that you live in. If you see something that you feel needs changing, what can you do to help bring about that change? We all carry more influence than we think.

We can change things one tiny step at a time by being the best we can be. If we make time for people, show them respect, help them when they need help then we can set an example and inspire others so that they can also become kinder and fairer to others. Children copy what they see. If they see you being caring and considerate then care and consideration will come naturally to them.

99. What can we learn from History?

Great things and terrible things have happened in the past. We can learn many lessons from History. If we look at the things that have gone wrong in the past we can take steps to avoid something similar happening again.

Equally we have lived through times of peace and abundance and we can look carefully at the principles that we lived by during those times and we can attempt to bring about those factors again.

People spend a lot of time looking at how they are different from other people and it is often these perceived differences that drive them apart and lead to wars but if we spend time examining the ways that we are similar then we are more likely to cooperate and learn from one another. Many books have been written about History. Reading these books is time well spent. Let us learn from the mistakes of the past and honour the successes.

100. Asking For Help:

While it is good to be able to do things for ourselves it is also important to recognise when we need help. Our families and friends can sometimes help but sometimes we need to ask for professional help in order to move on. Knowing when to ask for help is one of the most difficult things to do but it is so important. If we have health problems we sometimes need to seek medical advice and when we feel depressed we sometimes need professional counselling and support, for example.

Asking for help when it is needed is a positive step. There are a range of organisations that can help us. They range from statutory services to charities. There are life coaches and therapists that can help us to move forward. The important thing is to be informed. Find out what is available to you and then decide what is right for you.

I hope that you have gained from reading this book. We all deserve to live happy lives and once we realise that we are responsible for creating our own happiness our lives start to change for the better.

If you would like to find out more about what I do please visit my website:

http://www.trustylifecoaching.co.uk/

You can also contact me via my blog:

http://trustylifecoaching.blogspot.co.uk/

I would be very interested to hear your responses to this book and any ideas that you have to help others to create a happier life for themselves!

Printed in the United States
By Bookmasters